"This book has been missing from _____ for too long. People who are walk ___ a similar path to Rachel's will feel seen, known, and loved as they read these tenderhearted and gospel-centered pages."

Laurie Krieg, Author; Teacher; Hole in My Heart Podcast Host

"I thank God for Rachel Gilson. She has written a book that is both a biblically faithful and a very personal explanation of and rationale for what the Bible says about human sexuality. She writes to all of us, but especially to those who deal with the pain and confusion of same-sex attraction and sexual dysphoria. She knows this pain from the inside. So while she addresses these issues with theological carefulness, she does so with tremendous compassion, helping us to see that God's design for sexuality really is very good, merciful news."

Jon Bloom, Co-Founder and Board Chair, DesiringGod

"Rachel Gilson's life is a testimony to the sufficiency and power of the Scriptures. Her book is a testimony to a living faith that is based on that sufficiency and power. Rachel doesn't just read Scripture faithfully—she lives it faithfully too. And her book challenges me, likewise, to grow in my faith beyond a life of comfort and easy answers."

Karen Swallow Prior, Author, _On Reading Well_ and _Fierce Convictions_

"This book is worth reading just to learn about and rejoice in God's work through Rachel. But the book offers so much more, with rich biblical reflection on identity, marriage, singleness, romance, friendship, and more. Rachel's honesty and clarity make this book useful for sharing in so many diverse contexts, whether you're wanting to investigate Jesus and his gospel or you're leading in the church."

Collin Hansen, Editorial Director, The Gospel Coalition; Author, _Blind Spots_

"_Born Again This Way_ is a heartfelt, wise, and hope-filled book. In it, Rachel Gilson offers same-sex-attracted Christians and those who love them a Christ-centered and story-driven reflection on how to thrive in Christ. Not content to speak in generalities, Rachel delves into the practical everyday struggles of same-sex attracted Christians, speaking to questions about friendship, singleness, sex, and identity. The result is a warmly compassionate and theologically perceptive harvest of insights that will inform, challenge, and encourage the reader. Highly recommended."

Bruce Ashford, Professor of Theology and Culture, Southeastern Baptist Theological Seminary

"This is a brilliant book by a remarkable writer with an astonishing story and a decade of theological training. It offers no glib before-and-after narrative, but is a practical guide for sinners—same-sex attracted and otherwise—who dare to believe that Jesus is the best lover. I wish I could have given it to my younger self."

Rebecca McLaughlin, Author, *Confronting Christianity: 12 Hard Questions for the World's Largest Religion*

"Rachel Gilson masterfully and disarmingly presents a winsome narrative and a solid Christian theology of sexuality that is much needed in today's world. With so much confusion and polarization surrounding such issues, she offers a refreshingly honest perspective that is balanced and nuanced; there is lament and there is satisfaction, and amazingly they can coexist! Reading this book feels like you are sitting at coffee with her and that she cares for you."

Allen Yeh, Associate Professor of Intercultural Studies & Missiology, Biola University, Cook School of Intercultural Studies

"This book is a pastoral gold mine full of biblical advice for us all—movingly illustrated by the lives of Rachel and her friends. It wonderfully tells of how same-sex attracted people can both become Christians and stay Christian in a world which often believes that neither is possible."

Ed Shaw, Co-founder, livingout.org; Pastor, Emmanuel City Centre, Bristol; Author, *The Plausibility Problem / Same-Sex Attraction and the Church*

"This is a rich and unique contribution to the myriad stories of gay or same-sex attracted Christians who have committed to the counter-cultural truth that Jesus is Lord. Rachel Gilson explores the vital territory of God's good news about our desires, and demonstrates that, in Christ, our destination is to live in the greater satisfaction of holiness. As a same-sex attracted woman, Rachel's depiction of journeying through marriage with her husband, and of coming to know Jesus more deeply through her wrestle with sexuality, is a great gift and truly a must-read for all."

David Bennett, Author, *A War of Loves*; OCCA Research Fellow

RACHEL GILSON

BORN
again
THIS
WAY

thegood**book**
COMPANY

Born Again This Way
© Rachel Gilson, 2020. Reprinted 2020, 2021 (twice).

Published by:
The Good Book Company

thegoodbook.com | thegoodbook.co.uk
thegoodbook.com.au | thegoodbook.co.nz | thegoodbook.co.in

Published in association with Don Gates of The Gates Group,
www.the-gates-group.com

ISBN: 9781784983901 | Printed in Turkey

Design by André Parker

CONTENTS

"For they were not, as I saw it, my readers, so much as readers of their own selves, my book being merely one of those magnifying glasses of the sort the optician at Combray used to offer his customers; my book, but a book thanks to which I would be providing them with the means of reading within themselves."
Marcel Proust, *Finding Time Again*

FOREWORD

BY SAM ALLBERRY

One of my favourite moments in any James Bond movie is when "Q" turns up. Before Bond sets out into danger, he stops by the quartermaster to be given some latest piece of equipment or gadget. The scene normally provides a few moments of light relief before the intensity of the main conflict resumes. It is also a moment when we can guess something of what is going to happen in the rest of the film; because whatever Q gives Bond turns out to be exactly what he will need. If Bond ends up with a tall pepper mill that doubles up as a flame-thrower, we can be sure that at some point he's going to find himself in a pizzeria surrounded by evil henchmen. However weirdly specific the gadgets are, they will always be the exact thing he needs.

I'm confident that for many of us, this book will feel just like that. In some senses this is a niche book. Rachel is addressing issues experienced by only a subset of Christian men and women. That specificity will be a huge gift to readers who at last realize they are not alone in what they're going through. Yet the struggles Rachel addresses are also but one type of the battle faced by all who find themselves captivated by Jesus Christ, and her guidance and worked examples will apply to anyone.

Nearly twenty years ago I was confused and profoundly angry with God. This had been brewing for some time, of course, but the trigger had been that I was wrestling painfully with same-sex attractions and they didn't seem to be going away. When I'd turned 21, I'd said to myself that I wanted to be married with kids by the time I was 30. It seemed a noble aspiration: the sort of thing God would be pleased with me wanting. I wanted to be a godly husband and father, for marriage and family to be a means of service to God and blessing to others. And yet, as I hurtled into the latter part of my twenties, those hopes were becoming increasingly unrealistic.

The issue wasn't just timing. Ever since I had had any conscious feelings of intimacy and longing, they'd always been toward other guys. When I became a Christian, I assumed that those feelings would naturally subside and appropriate attractions to the other sex would take their place. The fact that this didn't happen left me confused and bewildered, angry with God for not doing what I took to be his job in all this.

What made it worse was isolation. I'd not yet felt able to share these quiet agonies with anyone else. My Christian friends knew nothing of what I was going through, and instead made regular gay jokes that made me very hesitant to open up with them. I was going through all this on my own. I didn't know anyone who wrestled with unwanted same-sex attraction—or even that such Christians might exist—let alone have people to process this with and learn from.

So I wish I'd had the book you now hold in your hands. Rather than the angry confusion of my own head, I could have had the compelling, elegant biblical wisdom that flows from Rachel's. This book would not have taken away the struggles I was going through, but it would have provided much-needed encouragement and strength. Rachel writes with honesty—at times searing, painful honesty—and yet there is nothing gratuitous or voyeuristic going on here. Rachel is simply helping us deal with real-life issues that too often go unaddressed. But more than that, Rachel writes with wonderful biblical clarity and insight. Many of the truths she's about to share have been hard-won—lessons learned the hard way. But, as she so beautifully demonstrates throughout these pages, all these truths have their origin in a God whose words to us are always and unfathomably good.

SAM ALLBERRY
Author, *Why Does God Care Who I Sleep With?*
and *7 Myths about Singleness*

WELCOME

I wrote this book for you, though only you know why you've picked it up.

I became a Christian much to my own surprise. It was as if the sun of the gospel had evaporated my atheism in an instant.

But as time went on, one reality remained like a stubborn puddle: I was sexually attracted to women. I still am.

So many questions pressed for attention. How could something that felt so right be condemned as wrong? Why would God prohibit acting on these desires for love? Would I ever have sex again? What words should I use to describe my experience—since neither gay nor straight seemed to fit? How should I navigate close female friendship in my new Christian community without everything getting… complicated?

My new Christian friends didn't know where to point me. They had never had to consider these questions from my angle; they were all attracted to the opposite sex—a fact which presented enough challenges of its own in the fight for joyful obedience. And all the while, we were bombarded with the loud, monotone <u>declaration of our culture</u>: "You must obey your sexual desires."

I remember one cool morning in Wyoming, sitting outside with a friend who also happened to be named Rachel. We were discussing one of our guy friends who had come to Christ in college. Before that, he had lived by following his own intuition of what would make him happy and fulfilled. He had had a girlfriend with whom he was sexually active, but when he met Jesus, he called it off and broke up with her.

Rachel and I had learned that this ex-girlfriend had recently also come to know Jesus as her Savior, and it seemed that she and our friend would now resume their relationship—this time both as Christians. Perhaps they would even one day marry! Wouldn't that be a lovely story of redemption?

It seemed like it to us. But it also made me quietly realize that that story would never be mine. If any of my ex-girlfriends came to Christ, I would rejoice. But none of them would be my future wife. Redemption could not look like that for me. It just felt so unfair: an ache in the heart that pulsed dreadfully, not letting me ignore it. I voiced it to Rachel and received sympathy. Yet neither of us really had an "answer." It felt like uncharted territory. It was.

Our culture sings that we're "born this way," as if that settles the matter. But I'm born again. My life has told a different story than what society expects for me and what I expected for myself, because God himself has written his own twists and turns into the narrative: unexpected blessings that are more powerful, more lovely, than anything I could have imagined in my former life.

This book is my story. It's just one among many, and it's not intended to be weaponized against anyone else or used as a pawn. But my hope is that my account of coming out, coming to faith, and what came next will be a refreshment to you on your own journey. Though I have experienced failure and pain, I have also received freedom and joy. In later chapters, I'll also share stories of others who are walking this path with their eyes fixed on the Lord.

Even more than stories, I want to offer you the Scriptures, and show you how those ancient, God-breathed words can meet us right in our very contemporary circumstances. They will challenge us and comfort us, and ultimately root us in the God who loves us.

And whoever we are, that's what we most need.

Maybe someone else pressed this book into your hands, hopes high for how it would impact you. Perhaps you're sure of your sexuality, but unsure of what Jesus has to say about it—or whether he has any right to own it. You are welcome here—I wrote this for you, even if you've picked it up secretly, with heart pounding, hoping no one will ask you why.

Maybe you find yourself secure in Jesus, fighting to say yes to him and no to same-sex sexual sin—yet still, like all Christians who have gone before us, you're living in a body that is not yet free from temptation. You don't want to limp to the finish line but to run your race with joy. This book is for you.

Or maybe you're listening in on this conversation as a pastor, significant other, friend, or parent of a Christian with same-sex attraction. You long to love like Jesus, who came full of grace and truth. This book is for you too.

I want to show you that Jesus is beautiful, powerful, and worthy right at the heart of this conversation, right at the heart of our sexuality. He is not scared or unsettled by anything, and if we are rooted in him, we can be people of power and love and self-control.

This is what I want for myself, and what I want for you. I'm not writing as a polished product, standing behind the finish line, clapping for you with the medal already around my neck. I'm right with you, sometimes stumbling, often aching, but also running with joy.

No matter where we start from, no matter what shape we're in, he is not hindered. His love and power are more than sufficient. He is always more than we expect.

CHAPTER 1

UNEXPECTED BIRTH

My treasure chest was heavy, and it burned in my hands.

There weren't rubies or gold pieces in the cardboard box. The valuables inside were heaps and heaps of paper and pictures: a catalogue of a former life. Printed out emails. Handwritten notes. Simple things outwardly, but like Gollum's ring in *The Lord of the Rings*, they claimed greedy possession of my heart.

Not that this obsession captured me every day or even most days. My life had changed radically from when those tokens had been gathered. I rarely thought about them in my comings and goings. Yet when I did encounter them, I was transfixed. They were all that I had left of my first romantic relationship with another girl. More than that, they were all that I had left of a former life. I could lose hours sifting and weighing, reliving and remembering. The box took me back to a time when my life resembled a binary star system, one sun being me and the other being her. In the years since, that life had become as distant as a galaxy. Why did I gaze at it? What promises could that dead system hold out to me?

You see, I had been transported to a new reality. I wasn't bearing the impossible weight of being in the center of my universe any longer. I was orbiting a new and better Sun. There was warmth and growth here—life I hadn't known before. I had never expected to find in Christianity such vitality, or to experience Jesus as a Savior and friend. Yet that was what he was. I found myself deepening my roots of faith and growing on a formerly foreign trellis.

But my occasional backward glances, my infrequent trips to the treasure chest, betrayed that my heart was still tied to my old life. It had held such power over me when I was a young adult, and that power still emanated from it when I turned my attention to it. I gave my allegiance to God, yes. But my old life begged for just a little room, just a little box. And I obliged.

Until, several years into my Christian faith, I made a new close friend. When she became aware of this box, she gently questioned the wisdom of keeping it. Didn't it only drag me backwards? Didn't it only glorify sin? Even now I feel my chest tighten as I recall her suggestion that I throw it all away. She didn't demand it of me, yet I felt defensive. I also felt her wisdom, the obviousness of the option.

So I sat one night, box in my hand, my heart ablaze as I considered these testaments to a life I had lived and loved—were they death or life for me?

In that moment it was as if I was reliving again my choice between two paths through life. I was choosing all over again, in some measure. What would I do?

———

By late high school, in the thick of that old life, I was hardening into my chosen identities. Academic success and love of reading made me think of myself as a budding scholar. Along with that came a firm rejection of Christianity. My limited interactions with Christians left me thinking of faith as intellectually feeble. It was like a sick dog that should be put down.

No, worse than that—it was a threat. An old dog can conjure up sentimental attachment. But in my eyes Christianity was not only stupid but cruel. I was culturally aware enough to have gotten the impression that Christians hated gay people. Hated them through legislation; hated them through signs waved. Hated them in jokes exchanged gleefully; hated them sometimes even in brutality. And for me this "them" wasn't theoretical. This "them" was me.

I discovered my attraction to women through one relationship in high school. Previous to that, I had had friendships with both sexes, and some romantic and sexual engagement with guys. Those interactions never seemed to live up to what my female friends talked about. I enjoyed friendship with guys, but their bodies seemed awkward in connection with my own. I reasoned that things would improve with greater experience. My household was not religious and didn't speak of sexual morality, and I assumed that it was good to experiment. After all, we weren't prudes.

It was indeed experience that shed more light, but not experience with a male. I fell in love with a girl, and desperately sought to connect with her romantically and sexually. With her

"Wasn't this what all the songs and movies were about? It felt as natural as hunger."

I finally felt what my peers had spoken of with their boyfriends: excitement and longing, fulfillment and joy.

When I first noticed this deep desire, I paused to wonder if it was ok. I had a sense that homosexuality—the only word

I had in my bank to describe it—was not accepted by most. Yet when I stopped to consider why, I couldn't for the life of me figure it out. Wasn't what I felt for this woman *love*—the thing that makes life worth living? Wasn't this what all the songs and movies were about? It felt as natural as hunger. I pursued it.

My relationship with her was exciting, consuming. It was also, as teenage relationships can be, tumultuous. At times when we had broken up, I would seek out the company of other young women. Each new encounter strengthened my conviction that my sexuality was at home with females, and in exile with males. I was running a science experiment, testing my same-sex hypothesis. All results confirmed it.

By the end of high school, I was convinced that everything central to my identity was opposed to everything central to Christianity. I was devoted to scholarship, to ideas, to truth. Christianity was about crutches, blindness, an autopilot life. I was determined to marry my girlfriend—it was the early 2000s, and legal gay marriage was about to emerge— and embrace my sexuality fully. Christianity was a cruel, nonsensical "No" to love in this form.

My choice of college was a declaration of my identity. Yale seemed as far away physically and ideologically from conservative small-town California as I could get. I felt that I was at the starting gate of my real life, and I was desperate to run.

It was right at that juncture that the Lord interrupted my path and redirected me.

I quickly learned at Yale that I was no longer the smartest in the room. I should have expected this. But I was hungover from the intoxicating experience of being an excellent student at a middling public school. Many of my fellow Yale students had spent formative years in places more suited to prepare for life at an elite college. And frankly, many were also just smarter. This injected a stiff shot of doubt into my view of myself.

While figuring out that terrain, my high-school girlfriend broke up with me. She left me for a guy who didn't deserve her, and I couldn't understand it. I was deeply in love with her, and the gut punch took me down right as my very first New England winter started to settle in. A type of cold and darkness I had never grown up with mirrored my new emotional state. I was unmoored from two main anchors that had previously held me: my intellectual prowess and my first love.

There was nothing in me that led me to think that I should turn to God. Instead I spent the winter break scrolling through other things to throw myself into. I wondered whether I should write for a school paper, or go to the gym more—anything that would occupy my energy and take my mind off of my failure, and help me to succeed again.

Early in that spring semester, I sat through a lecture on the 16th-century French philosopher René Descartes. He had constructed a philosophical argument for the existence of God which began with that famous phrase "I think; therefore I am." I thought it all sounded ridiculous. But somewhere in my mind a question pestered me: What if there was a God? I immediately rejected it. God was a false construct—unprovable, unsound. But this rebuttal couldn't shake that intrusive thought. It had been years since I had seriously considered the question of God's existence. Didn't it deserve another look, even if only to shore up my atheism with more mature supports?

Like a good millennial, I turned to the internet. There was freedom to type in any religious terms and see what came up. There was also privacy—I was ashamed of my interest. Sometimes a friend would enter my room, and I would slam my laptop shut, like a teenager caught with porn on the family computer. Nonetheless, I kept at it—and kept coming back to writings about Jesus.

Previously Jesus had always seemed like a cartoon to me—all bright lines, Caucasian features, and dull sayings. What I encountered instead was the depiction of a person who was intelligent and tender. The contrast between those different images stoked my interest. But I also had a growing suspicion that even if this was fascinating, it couldn't be for me. My sexuality seemed to be a fundamental barrier.

The only two people I knew at Yale who identified as Christians were two girls who were dating each other, and one was training to be a Lutheran minister. I went to them. They assured me that the conflict between Christianity and same-sex romance was based on a traditional misunderstanding and sent me away with a packet of information that would set the biblical record straight. I took it eagerly. As I read, its logic seemed natural, and I was ready to consent. However, when I looked up the Bible verses discussed, it didn't square. The interpretations looked like a misreading of what was plain in the Bible text: that same-gender sexual contact was forbidden by God.

I felt shame. How could I have been stupid enough to think that there really had just been a millennia-old mix-up? Then I was angry, because I didn't understand. I violently threw the packet into my cheap dorm trashcan.

Not long after, I was in the room of an acquaintance. She was grabbing some item, and as I waited for her in her entryway, I spotted her bookshelf. It featured a small volume called *Mere Christianity*. The author's name, C.S. Lewis, rang a faint bell, but I hadn't been raised on *The Chronicles of Narnia* so I couldn't place it. Nevertheless, I desperately wanted to read that book. So I stole it.

On February 12, 2004, I was about midway through reading the book in Yale's Sterling Memorial Library. Suddenly, I was arrested by the reality that there really was a God and that as our Creator he was the rightful judge of every person. I was afraid. My life thus far had been a parade of cruelty, lies, selfishness, and more. I was even holding a stolen book! Yet with that fear there rushed in a new, radiant understanding of Jesus Christ and his work: He had come and died and risen again so that

"I knew I would never get a better offer than what Jesus was extending to me, so I reached out my hand and shook."

God's wrath would be on him, and God's favor would instead rest on me. "[God] made him to be sin who knew no sin, so that in him we might become the righteousness of God" (2 Corinthians 5:21). A simple, terrifying, holy exchange. All I had to do was reach out and take it.

My mind raced with things that I sensed I must give up if I threw my lot in with Jesus: partying, finding a wife, control of my own life even. But how could these remain attractive in the face of overwhelming, undeserved mercy? Of salvation? Could I really pretend that the gospel was not true simply because it would be inconvenient for my life? That seemed the height of stupidity. I knew I would never get a better offer than what Jesus was extending to me, so I reached out my hand and shook. I closed my eyes and mumbled a prayer of repentance.

Then I packed up and went to class.

Within a week, I had discovered a Christian community at Yale. I immersed myself in their life together. They gave me a

Bible, taught me to read it and to pray, brought me to church, and introduced me to the dubious world of "contemporary Christian music." I found acceptance and joy. It was such a blessing to me that the first family of God I experienced were people who were academic and intellectually serious, because it shattered my long-held misconceptions about Christian thought life.

But none of this made a dent on my same-sex attractions. I don't think I had any expectations of what would happen in my sexuality; I was too focused on the newness of Christian life as a whole. As the months added up in my faith without change in those desires, I never felt ashamed of them. They were, after all, unchosen, and I was serious about saying no to what they demanded. I was mentally convinced of the *what* of my sexuality: to say no to same-gender sexual lust and actions. I had no access, however, to the *why*.

In this sense, I was obeying before I understood. To my mind, God's prohibition on same-sex relationships made no sense. My heart fully embraced the "love is love" narrative—the logical move from "God is love" to "People fall in love" seemed to validate all consensual romantic adult relationships. Weren't they all potential expressions of this higher reality? This seemed elegant and obvious. I wasn't craving murder or theft, but love, intimacy, and companionship!

I didn't understand; but would I trust him? Would I take as truth my word or God's?

This tension is as old as the Garden of Eden and is strong in the conversation around sexuality today. It is precisely where I felt on the knife's edge as a young believer. In the garden, God didn't make his first rule self-evident. And I think he didn't do that for a reason: so that we would trust in him, and not in our own understanding or execution of a rule. Let me explain.

God could have declared to Adam, *Don't murder Eve.* This would have been self-evident—I expect all of us would have nodded in approval. After all, taking life is gruesome and unjust. We feel naturally the sinfulness of killing. We would have looked on this statute and, using our reason and intuition, called it just. But we don't need to know God to make that judgment, and the vast majority of society can obey at least its outward form without relating to him at all. Its very obviousness renders God seemingly unnecessary.

So instead of giving those first humans a law that seemed obvious, God chose one that seemed odd. He told them that they could not eat of one particular tree in their richly appointed garden. Think about that: the law was to not eat a fruit. It almost sounds ridiculous—after all, even vegans eat fruit! How could there be anything immoral in it when it didn't even require an animal to die?

What is the motivation to obey a law that seems nonsensical? It can only be deep trust in the one who asks.

This is not how we relate to most laws though.

We have all felt flagging motivation when faced with apparently pointless rules. Who among us hasn't failed to fully stop at a stop sign, because we were the only ones at the intersection? Who hasn't told a little white lie to save face because no one would be hurt by such a small bending of the truth? Our moral code prizes "do no harm." It emphasizes the utilitarian spirit—what maximizes happiness for the greatest number of people? Putting a fruit off-limits doesn't pass our test. Neither does prohibiting certain romantic relationships.

When the serpent tempted Eve, he drew her attention to the apparent unfairness of the rule. He accused God of lying and withholding good from his people: "You will not surely die. For God knows that when you eat of [the forbidden fruit] your eyes will be opened, and you will be like God, knowing good and evil" (Genesis 3:4-5). Eve considered the data, and when she "saw that the tree was good for food, and that it was a delight to the eyes, and that the tree was to be desired to make one wise, she took of its fruit and ate, and she also gave some to her husband who was with her, and he ate" (v 6).

She looked at the fruit and saw that it was good, so she deduced that the serpent was right. God was withholding good from her. I looked at romance and sex between women, and it seemed good. Was God withholding good from me?

When we sit as judges over God's rules, we make ourselves God. We say, "I will be the one to determine if this is right. I am smart enough, trustworthy enough, to do so. I have what it takes to determine if this is a good rule or not." Just as with the stop sign at the deserted intersection, we make it only about the law itself, because we have no relationship with whoever installed it. But God's laws are not like an impersonal traffic code. They are like the words of a good parent. To go against a good parent when you're a child in their house is not just about an action, but about breaking trust between people.

I wonder if God didn't make his first rule self-evident because it would force Eve to consider: Did she trust him?

"I could trust God because in Christ he had proven himself trustworthy."

Was he that trustworthy parent? Hadn't he proven to her that he was for her good, so that, when confronted with confusion over his command, she could rest in the fact that his law wasn't arbitrary or cruel but somehow for her benefit?

In a similar way, when God's words about sexuality are not self-evident today—when they strike us as repressive—who will we consider more trustworthy: ourselves or God?

As a new Christian at Yale, this was not an idle question

for me. It pressed on a main hope for my future. It affected defining experiences of my life thus far. Could I trust God with even this? With such a vulnerable, important part of my life?

In Jesus Christ I found my answer: Yes. I could trust God because in Christ he had proven himself trustworthy.

After all, no one made him leave the glories of heaven. He was under no obligation to save us, to save me. He would be just as holy and good if I stood before him and was condemned in my sin. I had lived the first two decades of my life in arrogance, in lies, in cheating. I was cruel, selfish, and vain. Never did I think about the good of others, especially not ahead of my own. What did the God of perfect love owe a person like that? Exactly nothing. If I had gotten to the judgment seat still in my sin, and seen it exposed for what it was (and is) in the light of his goodness, I would have agreed with him: "You have to condemn me. You would be unjust not to." We feel the righteousness of a true criminal getting his due. So it would have been with me.

But instead, Jesus chose to come and rescue—"to seek and to save the lost" (Luke 19:10). The difficulty of the life he chose to live, even before his difficult death, showed how much we were worth to him. To take on a great cost shows great commitment and love. He was born to poor parents in the backwater of an oppressed, occupied country. His life wasn't spent traveling the world, seizing the moment. He wandered from place to place without a permanent home. His friends were often slow to understand and quick to bicker, and in the end they abandoned him. He was hounded by the religious elite, who should instead have worshiped him.

Despite the many difficulties, he poured out his life in love. He looked with compassion on crowds that chased him when he was exhausted (Mark 6:30-34). He spoke tenderly to women, healing and encouraging them (Mark 5:21-43; Luke 10:42). He took the risk to touch the contagiously sick

(Matthew 8:1-4) and to bless the outsider (Matthew 15:21-28). He wasn't afraid to be seen with sexually immoral women or morally corrupt tax collectors, but accepted them and set them free (Luke 7:36-50; John 4:1-30; Luke 5:27-32).

Jesus's life was exhausting, sorrowful—right to its end, as he submitted to shameful trial and execution. Jesus Christ, the Holy One of Israel, was strung up naked with criminals, covered in Gentile spit. He came of his own will to stand in for the debts of his people and pay it all. God showed that he accepted that payment by raising Jesus triumphantly from the dead. All are invited to exchange their sin for his righteousness and live forever with him.

This was my anchor when seas got stormy. I was free to obey before I understood because of *who Jesus is*, and who he had shown himself to be *for me*. Anything he said to me was for my good, even if I couldn't make out how. I could build my life on his goodness and love. I could echo the words the disciple Peter uttered as dozens of erstwhile followers abandoned Jesus because his teaching was so hard: that in this man I had come to believe and know the Holy One of God. He alone had the words of life (John 6:68-69). And that was enough, even with my remaining questions. Jesus was trustworthy; nothing he said would be arbitrary or a lie, but true and for the sake of blessing.

———

Years later, as I sat with the treasures and trinkets of my former life in my lap, I had to ask myself again, "Do I trust him?" What exactly was I holding on to with these papers? An emotional hit that God couldn't give? A sense of identity built on something that ran contrary to his will? Was my truest taste of love trapped in that long-gone time in my life? My clinging to the box testified that I still thought I knew best what love is, what love does.

Jesus is the true revelation of what love is and what love does. Had God not opened my eyes, I would have never seen him for who he is. Had God not continued to draw near to me, I never would have had the strength to follow my friend's advice.

But he had, and I did. In faith, I put each piece of paper into the recycling. That was who I was, not who I am.

The questions come for you too. Who is he? Who are you? Can you trust him?

CHAPTER 2

UNEXPECTED VISION

A good friend is willing to have the same conversation over and over again—and I really needed a good friend.

About four years after I became a Christian, Jane and I started to meet weekly at the local Starbucks to talk theology and sex. We were both young and educated at elite liberal universities. We were also evangelical—committed to God's word and ethic. We believed both in the melody of biblical faith and also the melody of academic reason. Sometimes those notes made beautiful music together. But in other areas they jarred the ear, making us jump in our seats.

That was often how it felt as we discussed sexuality. We knew that Jesus, our Savior, meant every one of his words to us to be for our good. So even in moments of frustrating confusion, it was with hope that we asked our never-ending questions. Is it true that "love is love"—that since God is love, two consenting adults loving each other cannot be wrong? Is God cruel if he denies someone romance? Why male-and-female marriage alone?

These questions weren't just a matter of idle curiosity for me. My new choices and my identity were staked on the answers. These questions probably aren't abstract for you either. You ask them, or someone you love does. It could be tempting, as you read in this chapter the conclusions that the Bible led us to, to lose sight of the years it took to embrace them, the anguish in asking. Let me assure you, we did not feel, contrary to the words of an old hymn, "peace like a river." We were more like Jacob in Genesis 32—wrestling with a stranger through a long night, demanding a blessing. And blessing is what we won.

———

Jane and I soon found that the subject of sexuality is everywhere in the Bible. True, there are just a handful of passages that prohibit same-gender sexual contact, but to reduce the Bible's teaching on sexuality only to those would be a mistake.

After all, we reasoned, you can't gain the full picture by looking only at the prohibitions. People trained in identifying counterfeit money don't need to know every type of forgery on the market. They need to be flawless experts in the real thing. Only then will their eyes catch the most sophisticated of fakes. We needed to train our eye on the positive vision for sexuality.

But where to start? Sexuality is a funny word, after all. It can refer to the reality and implications of biological sex, but also to the attitudes and actions around sexual attraction and behavior. No small topics, to be sure.

We decided we needed to go to the beginning, before sin entered the world. We needed to read Genesis 1 – 2, which is perilous precisely because none of us live in that world. Instead, our world groans under the disfigurement of human rebellion. Nor is the Garden of Eden the destination where God is taking his people. It was a good start, but it is not the finish. God is taking us instead to the new heavens and the new earth. So we need Genesis 1 – 2 to understand the world before sin, but we need the whole biblical story to see God's purpose and design for sexuality.

To not look at this in its entirety would be like taking eight different *Star Wars* novices and showing them each a different film from that franchise. If we then asked them, "What is the Force?" or "Who is Luke Skywalker?" given their limited view of the narrative arc, we would get wildly different answers—and all of them incomplete. The context of the whole story is key.

The view of sexuality from one end of the Bible to the other provides a positive image of three-fold blessing. "Blessing" can be a dusty religious term—you can blow it clean by thinking of it as a gift from God: a gift with spiritual meaning and power. Whether we're married or single, through the blessing of sexuality God communicates powerfully about three things: his prizing of diversity, his priority towards new life, and his love for his people.

———

Diversity is a buzzword in society at the moment, and with good reason—we grasp that if every thing or every person were the same, it would be to our loss. There is strength and beauty in difference. And when we value diversity, we're acknowledging the beauty of something *God designed*. We see the first notion of God's priority towards diversity right in the Garden of Eden in his purpose for humanity.

Genesis 1:27 is a small poem summarizing God's creation of humankind. It has three lines which build upon each other. Their similarity shows us their connection:

> *So God created man in his own image,*
> *in the image of God he created him;*
> *male and female he created them.*

God created humans; fine—but he also created lichen and pebbles. What sets us apart is that humans aren't just created, but created in God's image! Much ink has been spilled over the meaning of that statement. At very least, it must have some relationship to resembling God. That is a big deal, and in line two of this poem the statement is repeated and rearranged for emphasis. But the third line adds even more: sex difference is a key way that God's image is displayed in humanity.

The male and female sexes were not accidental. God could have created three sexes or one sex, but he made two. So even in the smallest community of humans ever—these first two persons—diversity was present. And not only that, but there was unity *because of* diversity, not in spite of it. Both of them together made up humanity—if one were missing, humanity would be incomplete. In this sense sexual difference could well be a dim reflection of the mystery of the Trinity: a way in which this image-bearing takes flesh.

The original pair in the garden don't just give us the pattern of diversity but are the ongoing source of it. All further human diversity (like the differences in our ethnicities or personalities) would enter the world through them through reproduction. As we trace the storyline of the Bible, we see that diversity in unity is a major feature of God's plan for humanity. Even when he called one man, Abraham, to be the father of a special people, the big vision was to bless "all the families of the earth" (Genesis 12:3). This was fully realized when "God sent forth his Son, born of a woman" (Galatians 4:4), to gather to himself a new diverse but unified people, paid for by Christ's own blood.

So sex difference is a key ingredient of the diversity that makes us human and blesses us. Even apart from the capacity for sexual union, there is glory, dignity, and purpose for us in being sexed. This shows up in single-sex scenarios and in mixed-sex ones. There can be a special bonding that happens when just women gather: a freedom and flourishing. Similarly, I've heard my male friends report a deep satisfaction that comes from men being with other men—something that feels instinctually correct.

And then there can be special joy and energy when the sexes are together as well. Respected polling entity Gallup reports that men and women work better together in business settings than either group working as single-sex units. Not all men and women fall into typical gender roles, yet there is a dynamism that emerges when both sexes work together. Perhaps that's why God designed the first team with an even gender split.

But the reality of the fall means that difficulty has entered even this primal aspect of humanness. Some of us don't feel the blessing of sex difference, because of the historic patterns of oppression that women have faced. Others struggle to feel internally aligned with their sex. Still others were born with intersex conditions, so determining their sex is more difficult than with most people.

There is hope in Christ for you—if you have felt alienated from your sex or have wrestled with the challenges of intersex, you will someday receive a new glorious body, and peace with it, having your tears wiped away. That doesn't mean present trouble will disappear, but Christ is very near to us in it while we wait for that day and look for help now.

There is hope in Christ for us all—he has come to restore all things. His new community is one where sexual difference is prized, with equal dignity for male and female. When the Holy Spirit first came upon the disciples, Peter proclaimed that the words of the prophet Joel had been fulfilled: "Your sons and your daughters shall prophesy" (Acts 2:17). Just as Adam and Eve shared the work they were given, brothers and sisters in Christ all share in God's work today.

In the new community of Christ in the future, all the nations will be gathered into one body. This diversity in unity has already begun, and it won't be complete until the end. It is so much more than sex diversity, but it is certainly not less.

Femaleness and maleness are key components of being human, and therefore of bearing God's image in the world; this is an extraordinary privilege. Thus the first blessing of sexuality comes through being sexed at all.

————

You might be noticing that all this sex talk hasn't even gotten to *sex talk* yet. But when considering the reality of the male and female sexes, that doesn't take long. The second blessing of sexuality comes from its capacity to create new life. Here we see the necessity of both sex difference *and* sexual union. It is sometimes said that where God commands, he always supplies—when he told Adam and Eve to be fruitful and multiply, he also built into their bodies the capacity to do just that. Neither could have done it alone, or with a partner of the same sex.

The process of reproduction is so familiar that we can lose sight of how grand it is. God is the unique Maker of life— only he can speak something out of nothing. But surely it is some capacity of our image-bearing that when male and female combine, we can create life too. And not just any life, like a microbe or a bacteria. No, our union creates a human soul who will last forever. The power of sex difference and sexual union is generative, explosive.

And it is indeed a blessing. God told Adam and Eve to fill the earth with humans because he loves us. Filling the earth with his image-bearers would bring order, life, creativity, and joy. On an individual level, the intimacy of bearing a child opens up new depths of self-sacrificial love and delight within us. We gain by experience a picture of God's parental love towards us—a new sense of what he means when he declares, "As one whom his mother comforts, so I will comfort you" (Isaiah 66:13), and "As a father shows compassion to his children, so the LORD shows compassion to those who fear him" (Psalm 103:13). God dignifies both fatherhood and motherhood by comparing himself to both roles (although certainly he uses male pronouns in his revelation and invites us to call him "Father"). Sex difference is required for procreation, and it is also honored in the roles it brings about.

So there Jane and I were, with oversized lattes and oversized Bibles crowding the small wooden table at the corner Starbucks, flipping pages and asking questions. We realized that even in all the goodness of procreation, men and women are never encouraged in the Bible to be fruitful and multiply outside of the bounds of marriage. This is not a machine-gun method, aggressively sending our genetic material into the world for the sake of the species. The family, centered on sex-differentiated marriage, is intended to be a bond of love, commitment, and durability, which supports the growth of children.

Cut to the sound of a scratched record. This pretty image doesn't match our world, does it? So many of us have an experience of family that is far from this cohesive unity. And many of us, even if we've grown up in families like this, may end up single through circumstance or choice as adults. Are we then cut out of the only human refuge of joy?

Not at all—because in the New Testament, the Genesis-1 command to "be fruitful and multiply" gets transposed— not obliterated—by Jesus's call to "Go and make disciples" (Matthew 28:19, NIV). Motherhood and fatherhood are imbued with new power and dignity because now they can be spiritual. It is not coincidental that becoming a Christian is called being born again.

This spiritual parenthood has distinct advantages. Its offspring cannot be taken away forever by death. It can produce much bigger families, since it is not limited by biology or resources. And like any great biological parent, spiritual parents leave a legacy of love.

And even spiritually, birth is best accomplished when new life is ushered into a family—the church family. This is a theme we'll explore in greater detail later. But it is worth mentioning

"The nuclear family is a temporary picture, while the church is permanent; it's the real deal."

here that the nuclear family is a picture, and temporary, while the church is permanent; it's the real deal. It is made of spiritual mothers and fathers, brothers and sisters who comfort, exhort, bless, rebuke, contend, provide, commit, and love. It is messy and unchosen, just as natural families are. In the church we see men and women, singles and marrieds, adults and children, with our big brother Jesus, the Holy Spirit uniting us, and worshiping our heavenly Father.

Church life is where we see most clearly the goodness of diversity—it displays the power of the Spirit to bring us together into something greater than each individual member. Standing and worshipping all together, we can feel that God's priority for diversity really is a blessing. It is *good* to be different, and united.

———

All of this points to the fact that marriage isn't just a vehicle for producing happy babies. It *is* the best context for children to be raised in, and children are one of its blessings. But we recognize that marriage is more than that too. We sense that it would be wrong to deny infertile couples the right to marry, or the elderly. What then is the "more" that marriage is for?

Our culture would answer that the more is made up of companionship and sexual pleasure. Movies, songs, TV shows, and literature all build a picture of a soul mate, a unique partner in life. We're told we can identify our soul mate by the way they make us feel, in our hearts and in our bodies. And it's not just something we're told about but something many of us have experienced—the intoxication of a strong interpersonal connection. Or we see that in other people and ache for it ourselves. In this way our legends and our lived experience team up as expert witnesses to plead their case: pleasure and partnership must be the "more" of marriage.

When we follow this line of thinking, we quickly observe that sexual difference is not required for either of those things. A man can deeply connect with another man romantically, emotionally and intellectually. A woman can find satisfying, joyful, erotic connection with another woman. Of course they can. So how could the Bible deny same-sex partners marriage when they have the main ingredients for it? Denial seems arbitrary and cruel.

A difficulty in rebutting this vision of the "more" of marriage is that the Bible *does* support sexual pleasure and companionship as goods built into marriage by God. He is the One who put a whole book in the Bible, the Song of Songs, about the goodness of sexual pleasure in marriage. He is the One who inspired the proverb "Let [one's wife's] breasts fill you at all times with delight; be intoxicated always in her love" (Proverbs 5:19). These are pictures of joy and marital indulgence. God gives good gifts to his creatures, which is why humans have the capacity for these intense connections at all.

But it is symptomatic of human sin and rebellion that we confuse God's good things with ultimate things. We always resist worshipping and honoring him. We prefer comfort to submission. So we take God's stuff and try to ditch God.

This is what is happening with the goodness of marriage. We see the parts we like—the trio of procreation, pleasure and partnership—and call this enough. And because we're image bearers with common grace, we can often build some decent things with these pieces alone—which is why, for example, same-sex relationships can display affection, health, and commitment. But because we're sinful, broken image-bearers, what we build with the pieces can never match the fullness that God intended.

It would be like building a car with an incomplete engine. Outwardly, it would still look like a car. It could roll and have seating. Yet a car cannot fulfill its purpose with half an engine. It's meant to be a powerful tool for distance transportation and fails if it only comfortably sits still. Similarly, marriage is meant to be a powerful tool for communication and fails if it doesn't deliver its message: the gospel.

The designed purpose of marriage is to illustrate metaphorically God's relationship to his people (as we'll see from Ephesians 5:22-33). And just as a car's engine is complex, and fails if it lacks a crucial part, so the engine of marriage is complex, and fails if it lacks a crucial part. A marriage cannot rightly depict God's relationship with his people if it lacks faithfulness, or pleasure, or fruitfulness—or sex difference. The metaphor demands it.

———

This returns us to our original pursuit: understanding God's positive vision of sexuality in the Bible. The first blessing of sexuality is the way it shows us the priority God gives to diversity, which is both highlighted in and sustained by sex difference. The second blessing of sexuality is the gift of children, a fruit of both sex difference and sexual union. And the third blessing of sexuality is that it creates the possibility of marriage as a picture of God's relationship with his people— and that picture specifically requires sex difference.

God didn't look down from heaven on human marriages

and think, *Huh, that kind of looks like my relationship with my people. I should use that.* No. He knew that we would need help to understand what his love for us is like, and what our obligations are to him, and so he created marriage to act as a metaphor. Marriage has been practiced across cultures and throughout time, which only goes to testify that it points to something greater than itself.

We've already thought about how the parent-child relationship similarly teaches us something about God. And there, God does not shy away from either father imagery or mother imagery. That makes it especially noteworthy that when God speaks of himself and his people being "married," God is *always* the male, and his people are always the female. Take, for example, Isaiah 54:5-6:

> *For your Maker is your husband,*
> *the LORD of hosts is his name;*
> *And the Holy One of Israel is your Redeemer,*
> *the God of the whole earth he is called.*
> *For the LORD has called you*
> *like a wife deserted and grieved in spirit,*
> *like a wife of youth when she is cast off,*
> *says your God.*

The imagery is even clearer and more intentional in Ephesians 5:22-33, where the husband is said to represent Jesus Christ and the wife represents his church.

Why does sex difference matter for the metaphor? By constructing marriage to be made up of two members who are inescapably different, God teaches us at least three things about his relationship with his people.

First, the relationship by definition can't exist without both parties. So if you lack one of the partners, you destroy the picture. Lose the male from the marriage, and you lose the picture of Christ. Lose the female, and you lose the picture of the church. The love story of redemption is about both of these parties, so they must both be represented. Second, the members are not interchangeable—Christ is not the church, and the church is not Christ. We have different roles and responsibilities within the one shared relationship; hence the same is true in marriage. Third, the male and the female are different from each other yet able to be united because of shared humanity. So too, God and his people are essentially vastly different. But because of the work of Jesus, who is both fully God and shared in our humanity, we and he are able to be united. There is mystery here, and miracle.

We still may ask why the difference has to be sex. Aren't there other kinds of very meaningful differences, such as personality type, which could perform the same function of picturing the difference and unity of Christ and the church? So, for example, an analytical no-nonsense man could provide clarity and strength for his more emotionally intelligent male partner, while the latter brings joy and vibrancy to the former.

We would be naive to assume other types of difference don't matter, or don't contribute beautiful things in our various relationships. But there is something about sex difference which sets it apart from other kinds. It is both "large scale"—usually identifiable from just the briefest of glances—and also written into the smallest parts of our cells. A traumatic brain injury could completely change my personality, but nothing can truly change the reality that I am female. The gospel is about an uncrossable chasm shockingly bridged. We are made in God's image, yet he is also completely other. Males and females are equally human yet inescapably different from each other. The metaphor's power is in showing love across a fundamental, primary difference.

The metaphor also explains why procreation, pleasure and partnership are such meaningful pieces of marriage. Jesus's union with his church is supposed to be fruitful, and procreation is a picture of that. His union with his church is intimate and enjoyable, hence in marriage we experience the pull of sexual pleasure. His union with his church is safe and secure, thus marriage provides the joy of faithful companionship. This trio of "goods" is designed to maximize the goodness of the union as a whole, and they all drive us back to the main thing: marriage is a metaphor for non-interchangeable entities in an intimate relationship: Jesus Christ and his church.

There is power in the picture. But again, in Christ, marriage has been transformed. It is still a valid picture. Yet it remains *only* a picture. God is not cruel to deny some people romance, because this is only one of the pictures God has drawn to show the gospel. It is a powerful one, and we are right to long for it—it connects to the longing we should feel for him. Yet whether or not we have the earthly model, if we are in Christ, we forever have the real thing.

The real union has started and is coming. When the new heavens and the new earth are ushered in, we won't need the sign any more. We will have arrived at the destination: the

"Whether or not we have the earthly model, if we are in Christ, we forever have the real thing."

wedding feast of Jesus and his bride. Singleness is therefore filled with fresh dignity. Single Christians communicate that a truer marriage is coming and that they are willing to bet their life on it. They communicate that the church really is a family, and we better live like it. Even when his singleness is unchosen and painful, the single man communicates how much Jesus longs for his wife, the church. The single woman shows the longing of the church away from the LORD: how worth waiting for he is. And neither will feel as if they have missed out when the picture is swallowed up by the real thing.

———

It wouldn't be fair to say that Jane and I got to all of these things on our many coffee dates. But it was the place where I solidified the realization that God's sex ethic wasn't primarily a bunch of "no's." God designed sex difference, and sexual union, for some very big "yes's". Yes to diversity. Yes to new life. Yes to relationship with God through Jesus Christ. Our popular culture reflects our instinct to communicate about sex; and God has designed sex to communicate about big, beautiful things.

When we rebel against him, as we all do, we scramble the signal. We must repent and believe in the gospel. But even when we do, even years after we surrender to Jesus, we may sometimes have a hard time tuning in to the message of God's goodness; we twist the dials and hear only white noise. I have certainly felt like that in the past. Maybe you feel like that right now. Maybe you still struggle to see the goodness in the metaphor, or its necessity, especially in the face of powerful desire.

Do not despair. Take this blessing as your own: "May the God of peace himself sanctify you completely, and may your whole spirit and soul and body be kept blameless at the coming of our Lord Jesus Christ. He who calls you is faithful; he will surely do it" (1 Thessalonians 5:23-24).

But even this raises our next question: Does sanctification for us mean becoming straight?

CHAPTER 3

UNEXPECTED OPTIONS

"You have to end it."

If this phrase had been wielded like a blade, what would my heart have done? Or if it had thudded to the floor, heavy with ultimatum, would my flesh have rebelled?

I'll never know. Instead it was carried to me on tears, through pleading eyes and a quiet voice. The full force of a friend's love was behind it, and I knew it was true. And not only true, but good.

I had not yet been a Christian for a full year. I sat across from my friend Sylvia on her dorm room bed. The early December evening was dark outside her window. For ten months, Sylvia had served as my gentle guide into Christian life. I entered our campus ministry unarmed with evangelical mores or manners. My first steps into community were stumbles, especially in terms of language choice and drinking. Sylvia was not one to rebuke. Her tactics were to keep turning me toward the good, and offer helpful distraction. If there has ever been a human who has felt safe, Sylvia was that person.

A few weeks into my faith, I drank too much at a party. I called Sylvia as I left. She would have had a right to correct me, to explain that that is not how Christians should act—I was under age and I had had too much even if I wasn't. Instead, she told me to meet her at her dorm, and we walked around campus for what felt like hours, talking, getting me sobered up.

So months later, in that December when Sylvia implored me to "end it", her words were unshakable, full of authority.

What she said I had to end was my relationship with a girl. I'll call her Anna. I had met her in the late spring after coming to Christ. We had an instant, undeniable connection. She was spending the summer in New Haven, just as Sylvia and I were, and as I got to know her, I fell in love. Despite knowing better, I allowed that love to express itself physically. It simply felt too overpowering to deny. I had thought that no other human could get me like my high-school girlfriend; suddenly Anna came in and showed me that I was wrong.

Yet I was also convinced that same-sex sexual relationships fell outside of God's design, and I desired to honor him.

I spent months pinging between these two deep desires, bouncing off the wall of one across to the other. Each time I struck a wall, a piece of me hardened or chipped off. Even more, I compounded my sin by lying, keeping my patterns in the dark. So in the fall I would go to worship-band practice and then scoot off to Anna's room afterwards.

Being with Anna was not merely sexual. It felt like coming home. But the Holy Spirit refused to let me go. He created unease, bringing the word to bear in my mind. He caused me to ask, in scenes where my flesh felt satisfied, in moments when my heart was full of connection with her: was this all it was cracked up to be? I had a growing awareness that I had to walk away from this relationship for the sake of my soul. Jesus said that if someone loved him, they would obey his commands (John 14:15). To continue in disobedience was to betray my love of Christ.

And yet I felt I had no power in myself to leave.

———

How could I be caught between such contradictory desires? On the face of it they should have been mutually exclusive of each other. Yet maybe you too know how it feels to be torn between two camps. Your pull toward something forbidden feels as strong as a super-magnet. But it doesn't extinguish your opposite pull toward Jesus, your real desire to honor him. You feel that you could be ripped down the middle.

While the experience is alarming, God's word assures us that it's a challenge which is normal for the Christian. James 1 paints a portrait of these conflicting desires, and outlines two responses and two very different results that follow:

> *12 Blessed is a man for having withstood trial, for having withstood the test he will receive the crown of life, which is promised to those who love him. 13 Let no one say when tempted, "I am being tempted by God." For God is untemptable by evil, and he tempts no one. 14 But each one is tempted when by his own desires he is lured and enticed. 15 Then after desire has conceived, it gives birth to sin, and when the sin is full grown it brings forth death. 16 Do not be deceived, my beloved siblings. 17 Every good gift and every perfect gift is from above, coming down from the Father of lights, with whom there is no change or shadow from turning. 18 Willingly, he birthed us by the word of truth, so that we might be a kind of firstfruit of his created things. (James 1:12-18, my translation—as are all quotes from James 1 in this chapter)*

There is more in these words than we can cover right now. However, the broad view of this passage is the contrast between the person who has withstood trial and is blessed, and the person in danger of failing, in danger of experiencing death. God has given us this passage so that we would grow in our ability to be the first kind of person (v 12) and not the second (v 14-15).

———

If we're to understand what James is saying here, the first concept that needs to be unpacked is that of desires (v 14-15). It's a word which is important in the conversation around sexuality. We know from experience that humans can desire neutral, good, and wicked things. Desiring a turkey sandwich is not the same as desiring a friend's salvation in Christ, and different altogether than a desire to lie. The type of desire determines our response it. So what kind of desires is James talking about—are they neutral, good or wicked? And where does our same-gender sexual desire fit?

One key way to answer these questions is to look at the context. Verse 14 is clear: each person is tempted *when* they experience luring and enticing desires. That in itself is not necessarily sinful: I can be enticed by a cupcake if I'm in the right frame of mind, which is not automatically sinful but neutral. So is that the kind of "temptation" covered here? No—verse 15 shows us that it is desire *for sinful things* which James is discussing, because he employs a vivid metaphor for the cycle of sin. These luring desires, if they conceive, give birth to sin. That is where they will take us. That is why they are so dangerous for us. The desires being spoken of in this text are the desires for sinful things.

All this means that this passage has lots to say about our desires for same-gender sexual contact, because Scripture is clear that this is a desire for something sinful. The desire itself is not neutral but dangerous.[1]

---

1 The desires James talks about are otherwise unspecified—the precise things being desired are unnamed. This is in fact the normal pattern of usage in the Greek New Testament. The word behind the English "desire" here in James is *epithumia*, which can refer to desire both for good or for evil. However, in its 38 uses in the New Testament,

———

But if we dig a little deeper, we see that James' stark warnings also contain good news for those who feel same-sex attraction. First, the "desire" of sinful things is a broad category, which means James' warning is not for just some of us. Every person is vulnerable; every person faces their own cocktail of enticing desires. For those of us who experience same-sex attraction, the desire for romance and sex with people of our own gender will entice us to sin. Alongside that we'll also face a number of other desires that seek to draw us away, as every Christian does. James 1:13 says, "Let no one say *when* tempted...", not "*if* tempted." We are not alone in having to fight a battle against desire for sin. It's a normal part of the human condition—even the Christian condition.

Second, while some in our culture are obsessed with pinpointing a specific psychological, social, or genetic source of same-sex attraction, the Bible points to a spiritual source of *all* desire that is contrary to God's will. That it is spiritual doesn't mean that it isn't also "natural"—that is, something innate in us. In fact, the two are linked. Ephesians 2:1 declares that we were dead in trespasses and sins. We were each born with a spiritual inheritance of sin from our first parents. This spiritual state in turn makes us "by nature children of wrath," as Ephesians 2:3 continues, who slavishly chase our desires. Natural doesn't automatically mean good, therefore. We may well have been "born this way," but every one of us was born sinful.

---

only three refer to something positive being desired. And in each of those three cases, the positive thing desired is explicitly stated. For example, in Philippians 1:23 Paul states that he desires to be with Christ.

There is an entirely different pattern for the remaining 35 uses of *epithumia*. Each of these negative uses of desire leaves the object of desire unstated. The closest thing to specificity is in Mark 4:19 where Jesus warns of desires for "other things" which choke the word, or in Revelation 18:14 when the world is being judged, and the metaphorical "fruit" which they desired is no more. The word *epithumia* is used by Paul, Peter, James, John, and even Jude in this undefined but dangerous way. This clear pattern indicates that James is speaking of dangerous desire for evil things in our passage.

Knowing this is wonderfully freeing. Some people say they know where their attractions came from, but in reality most of us can't explain why they emerged, unchosen and unasked for. Nor do we need to. God doesn't ask us to explain the history and occurrence of each desire for sin—he explains for us that humanity has a natural, fallen condition to desire evil. Rather, he calls us to resist temptation and choose holiness, by the power of the Holy Spirit.

To do that, we need to understand the pattern of sin.

———

Most of us remember the image from high-school sex-education class of a female ovum being swarmed by myriad tiny sperm. Reproduction begins with that one sperm that combines with the egg to produce a human life. Consequently, the way to ensure that no child is conceived is to prevent the sperm from accessing the egg. Once the process begins, it can't but help press toward its goal of life as the cells divide and multiply. The picture in James 1:15 capitalizes on this sense of the inevitability of the reproductive process: "Then after desire has conceived, it gives birth to sin, and when the sin is full grown it brings forth death." In a perfect twisting of the image, sin presses not toward life but death.

One shouldn't press a metaphor too far, but it doesn't seem unfair to point out that it is easier to prevent conception than it is to stop a full-grown opponent from taking you down. When sin is full grown, it brings forth death—but death is only the final form of misery. Playing with sin now and thinking you can finish it off in the future is not only unwise but deadly. James paints this picture so we can be wise and nip our sin in the bud.

But what does that look like exactly? If stopping conception is wise and smart, we must certainly fight these desires for same-gender romance and sex. But does that mean seeking to become straight: replacing homosexuality with heterosexuality?

The Greek word behind "desire" in James is *epithumia*. While James doesn't give any specific direction about what to do with or to these dangerous desires, elsewhere the Bible tells us plenty. For example: Don't let sin make you obey its *epithumia* (Romans 6:12); don't gratify the *epithumia* of the flesh (Romans 13:14). If you live by the Spirit, you won't gratify the *epithumia* of the flesh (Galatians 5:16). Put off the old self, which has deceitful *epithumia* (Ephesians 4:22). Flee *epithumia* (2 Timothy 2:22). Don't be conformed to *epithumia* (1 Peter 1:14). Don't live for *epithumia* (1 Peter 4:2). In the strongest terms, Paul writes in Galatians 5:24 that Christians have crucified the flesh with its passions and *epithumia*, and in Colossians 3:5 he tells Christians to put evil *epithumia* to death, along with sexual immorality and other things.

What do we make of this? Is the strength of these words a command to replace homosexuality with heterosexuality? What about all the Christians who love Jesus and have seen no change in this part of their lives despite desperately trying to "pray the gay away"? What about the Christians who *do* report lasting change in their sexual desires? In later chapters we'll return to these questions as we hear from people with different experiences.

For now, at very least, we need to recognize that this is not a game. Everywhere God commands that we move completely away from any desire for sinful things. We seek the death of these things if we are in Christ. Simply replacing homosexuality with heterosexuality does not guarantee faithful living. It may simply change the object of lust. After all, there is an abundance of heterosexual sin in the church.

Fighting these desires could mean a change in attractional patterns for some. But it is crucial to note that that is never presented as the goal in any text, including this one. The goal is to faithfully say no to these desires—a willingness to crucify them, not coddle them. A crucified enemy may still spit threats from its cross, but it no longer has true power. Perhaps my attractional patterns will never change—they haven't these past 15 years, and many others report no change. That does

"In Christ I have the power and the obligation to say no to temptation and yes to God."

not undermine the fact that in Christ I have the power and the obligation to say no to temptation and yes to God. We are never promised relief from the presence of dangerous desires, but we are promised power to fight victoriously (1 Corinthians 10:13).

———

When it came to me and Anna in my sophomore year of college, I was well into the cycle of sin James talks about. Desire had conceived and produced sin, and it was difficult to get out. My attachment to Anna was only growing, like a healthy but malicious child. When Sylvia told me, "You have to end it," there were no truer words that could have been said. And no words more helpful.

In the moment of battle, I didn't need shame heaped on me for being stuck in sexual sin, or for having disordered desire in the first place. I needed support in the fight. Focusing on what to do because of who I now was in Christ was my key to faithfulness. Naming my sin to my friend was the first step in that battle, because sin loves to grow in secrecy. In subsequent days we made a plan. The severity of my attachment to Anna was such that I needed to just cut it off entirely. While we could theoretically have remained friends, this was simply not practically possible for me—the romantic and sexual elements of the relationship were too strong. The idea of ending it filled me with agony; but I knew it needed to happen.

Perhaps you too are convinced that similar desires need to be put to death. But what if you're trying and it simply feels too difficult? How could God expect us to have strength for this kind of battle? We often feel ready to give up the fight.

I loved Anna. It was a terrible feeling, abandoning the relationship with her. Because this feeling is so powerful, it can be the precise place where we rebel against God. James helps us avoid this tendency by highlighting two ways in which faulty thinking may lead to rebellion. The first is explicit; the second, implicit.

First, there can be the tendency to blame our desires or our situation on God. That way it's his fault, not ours. In James 1:13 the hypothetical tempted person declares that God is the one tempting them. James dismisses this by declaring twofold truth: God is untemptable by evil, and he tempts no one. He never desires evil, so it cannot tempt him; and he does not desire for anyone to sin, so he does not tempt them to do so. James says that when we are tempted, it is because of our own desire—and since that is so, we must take responsibility. Yes, God allows us to live in this world filled with temptation. He allows our faith to be tested. But his desire and his command are that we stand firm.

Perhaps you've heard a modern version of this blame shift. Our culture says that all sexual expression and desire is good and right, as long as there is consent. If you feel it, do it! So we conclude, "I feel these desires sincerely. I didn't ask for them, therefore they must be from God. God doesn't make mistakes." This is just a different way of shifting the burden to God. Saying that these desires are from God simply because they exist is a confusion between God's perfect will—what he desires actively for humanity—and God's permissive will: that which he allows given the circumstances of redemptive history. He is clear throughout Scripture that our desires are not a compass for goodness because they are broken. He is the compass for goodness, and he tells us plainly what pleases him and what will result in our thriving.

This gets us to the second, implicit, reason why we rebel against God. It's that sex and romance feel so good (except when they feel awful, which is a different topic altogether…). We see it in movies, in our friends, in our own life, and we say, "This is a good and perfect gift." And we are half right, which may be the most difficult type of right there is.

We are half right because, as we saw in chapter 2, God is the designer of marriage and sex, and he gave them to us precisely to bless us and to tell us truth about himself and us. But we are wrong when we wrench the gift out of his hands and use it against its design. One of the reasons why cancer is so insidious is that it takes a healthy, good function of the cell—reproduction—and directs it toward unhealthy ends: a vigorous reproduction of cells that puts the body in danger. Cancer doesn't change the power of the cell, but it changes the purpose. Likewise, when we co-opt sexuality away from God, we don't remove its power. God built that directly into it. But we can destroy its purpose, to deadly and devastating effect. This is especially true with same-sex romance, because the lack of sexual difference in the partnership completely obscures the picture God intends for sex to carry, and instead turns it inward. The picture becomes one of idolatry, not true worship.

This is why James warns us sternly in 1:16: "Do not be deceived." When something is powerful and radiates a remnant of goodness, it can sweep us off our feet. This is exactly what happened with me and Anna. The pulse of our relationship was strong. It felt too alive to kill, as if it was immortal. My desire had birthed sin, and it was a robust, attractive, and fierce opponent. In my natural self, I was outmatched.

But if sin has a life cycle, so does righteousness—and its parent is stronger.

───────

This passage from James tells the story of two birth plans in competition. The first mother is our own *epithumia*. In a sick twist, she wants to use birth, the entry point of life, instead as the entryway to death. This mimics our distortion of God's good gifts, when we use them for our own ends instead of his.

But God is opposed to both death and distortion. Though he had no obligation to rescue us, he chose to give us birth out of his own will (v 18). And the manner and purpose of his parentage give us strength to stand against our enemies.

First the manner: we are told that he gave us birth by his word: "the word of truth." We know that in the beginning, God created everything by simply speaking. We also know that Jesus, famously called the Word, is our Savior. His life, death, and resurrection clears us of sin, gives us his perfect righteousness, and unites us to himself forever. Not only that, but we have been given God's Holy Spirit, along with his sword, the Bible, to guide us in all faith and practice. These are the very words of God, in line with his powerful word of creation and indestructible Word of redemption.

Our desires whisper lies in our ears. They gather steam from our culture and shout over any objections. For those of us who experience same-sex attraction, the danger is very real. Every piece of our culture is going out of its way to affirm that impulse that exists unchosen in us. Everywhere we turn, someone is telling us that freedom is found in obeying these desires. Sometimes the voice even comes from those we trust most in this world: those who claim to love God.

We need God's words more than ever. He has not abandoned us to be raised in the orphanage of desire. He has given us birth, and given us in the Bible a vision of the goodness of our bodies. A vision for the real reason why sex is so powerful. A vision for his plans for it, and for us, in the world. It's a vision in which we don't have to become straight; nor do we have to inhabit being gay. We are free to use our bodies as the good gifts they are designed by their Creator to be.

This leads us to the purpose of our birth: to "be a kind of firstfruits of his created things" (v 18). Firstfruits were an offering to the Lord in Old Testament times: the earliest and best portion of crops, which was a big deal in an agricultural society. They were a holy declaration of thankfulness and expressed trust that God would continue to provide. And they were costly: the very best, the very first, was required. But that only increased the beauty and value.

If you are a Christian, this is the call God has put on your life. Not just a piece of it but the whole thing. When you submit your whole life to him, in thankfulness for what he has provided for you in Jesus, it is a holy offering—and God delights in it! But that doesn't mean it's easy. For those of us

"When I left Anna, it was agony every day for months. Yet it was completely worth it."

with same-sex attraction, denying those desires will feel like death, because it is. When I left Anna, it was agony every day for months. Yet it was completely worth it, just as Jesus had promised that we would gain our lives only by losing them.

This death must occur, often daily, so that the life God has purposed for us can come to full flower. As the Puritan theologian John Owen famously wrote, "Be killing sin or it will be killing you." Or as Sylvia less famously told me, "You have to end it." Our same-sex attraction may linger until we die or Christ returns. But until that day we have his power, his word, and his vision for a new way forward, because it is our birthright. We obey him, not our sinful desires. They are strong, but he is stronger. They make deceitful promises, but his promises are as firm as they are beautiful.

> *Blessed is a man for having withstood trial, for having withstood the test he will receive the crown of life, which is promised to those who love him. (v 12)*

As we move forward, we will see that this battle is never easy. Stewarding our sexuality is about faithfulness to Jesus, which is so much more than exchanging one set of attractions for another—in many ways this is much harder, but ultimately it is much more beautiful. We will see in the next chapter that we same-sex-attracted Christians have a unique and powerful ministry today when we fight for this faithfulness in our lives. But we will also see that this fight is worth it—because Jesus is worth it, and we are worth it to him.

CHAPTER 4

UNEXPECTED MINISTRY

"What are you going to do if she kisses you?"

The question made me indignant and embarrassed. Anita was a trusted friend, a woman who always saw right through me. She was twenty years my senior and, like me, had come to faith at Yale. Thoughtful and passionate about discipleship, she jumped right to the worst-case scenario.

I was going to take the train down to Manhattan to visit my high-school girlfriend. It was December 2005—a full year since Sylvia had confronted me about Anna. A full year of growth in maturity, surely. Wasn't my spine steeled to now be friends with my ex?

Our relationship had been rocky since my conversion in February 2004. I came to Christ while she and I were broken up, but two weeks later she called me. She said that ending it had been a mistake—we should get back together. It was all my heart had wanted. Yet I explained to her that I had become a Christian; I couldn't be with her anymore. There was deep anger and confusion, with insults and pleading. She had respected me for my intellect. Ideas had been such an important part of our bond. Wasn't defecting to Christianity the denial of a thinking life? And wasn't rejecting her love turning me into one of the bigots we had scorned together?

It was so hard to resist her. Many days I had longed for our old relationship again, its potency still in the air like lingering perfume. But by the grace of God I hadn't run to her—then or since. Sure, I had disobeyed with Anna, and in other ways. But wasn't my dedication to Christ shown in my refusal to go back to my ex? Despite other failures, that was a line in the sand I'd never cross, a golden calf I would not worship.

In the summer of 2005, I'd tried to establish a new, healthy pattern of relating to her. Perhaps I could love her like Christ, I thought. She'd experienced some hard things recently, and over the fall semester we talked and corresponded more and more. I felt that I was in a new place with her, that our closeness was now safe. That I was really helping her, and honoring God.

So, that night in December, as Anita and I stood in a hallway at a campus Christmas party and I casually told her about my overnight plans, I expected approval. Wasn't I being a great witness?

Her immediate, direct eye-contact question told me otherwise: "What are you going to do if she kisses you?" This was a battle-plan sketch, not an affirmation. In an instant, I knew I wasn't ready. Yet my very unreadiness was because I had let my heart become tangled up again. I used that knot of secret affections to shove down the revelation.

"That's ridiculous. It won't happen."

"But what will you do *if it does*?"

I was about to find out.

"For this is the will of God, your sanctification" (1 Thessalonians 4:3). Whether I knew this specific verse as the train pressed me toward New York, I don't recall. I do recall that as I turned

Anita's question over in my head, I felt no will to fight. The train was rushing me to the city, but my flesh was rushing me to sin. I lost the battle on the way, like an army sabotaged from the inside.

I had been a Christian for almost two years, growing in the joys of God and his community. Surrounded by his gifts, I

"The train was rushing me to the city, but my flesh was rushing me to sin. I lost the battle on the way."

gave myself to an old lover—I can scarcely write it without tears. I remember waking that night, watching the snow fall out the dorm window, feeling heavy for what I'd done with the girl next to me. And then choosing to do it again.

"For this is the will of God, your sanctification: that you abstain from sexual immorality." There was no hiding from my sin and disobedience. I knew full well what I'd done. That night didn't teach me that sexual immorality was wrong—I'd already been convinced of that. It did teach me that I was more treacherous than I had previously known.

And though it's a deep stain on my life of discipleship, God was able to take what I meant for evil and turn it for good. That doesn't for a moment excuse my decisions. Only by the grace of Christ was I able to take hold of confession, repentance, forgiveness, and restoration. But in the pit of disobedience, I had a sense of what I would forfeit if I walked away from my faith. That grew eventually, like a pearl that takes years of irritation to form, into a realization that same-sex-attracted Christians have unique and powerful ministries—that is, we serve the church and the world through our example of obedience.

How so? Because we witness powerfully to the beauty of Jesus over romance. Because we embody the necessity of relying on him alone to choose holiness. And because we prophetically call the church to honor God and neighbor by neither taking away from nor adding to God's word on sexuality. That's what we'll see in this chapter.

———

For this is the will of God, your sanctification: that you abstain from sexual immorality; that each one of you know how to control his own body in holiness and honor, not in the passion of lust like the Gentiles who do not know God.
(1 Thessalonians 4:3-6)

Isn't it interesting that Paul is able to equate holiness with refraining from sexual immorality? We know from a full reading of the Bible (not least, from Paul's own writings) that holiness is more than this. And yet there is something so important about our bodies, something so powerful about sex, that our sexual morality can act as a gauge for our discipleship. A high temperature isn't the only thing wrong with our body when we have a fever, but it is a sure sign that we're sick.

Whenever we see a text like this, our moralism can kick in. We want to prove that we're "good Christians," so we white-knuckle our way to obedience for a time. Or, in a rare moment of honesty, we feel the weight of how impossible obedience is, and in despair we run from God.

This was precisely the place I was in the next morning, with my ex. I was drowning in multiple waves of turmoil. My wickedness threw in my face that I was not as far along in obedience as I had thought. For all my church attendance, "quiet times," and theological reading, my heart had bolted like a scared deer when it came time to choose the good.

Hiding behind self-righteousness was not a possibility for me that morning.

Running away, however, was a live option. No one in my Christian community yet knew what had happened; I was miles away. As my ex and I walked arm in arm around snowy Central Park, I imagined what it would be like to leave everything I had built in the past 22 months. Surely my roots weren't so deep as to not be pulled up? When I went back to Yale, I could simply stop attending church and stop seeing my Christian friends. I could dive back fully into my many non-Christian friendships and rekindle my natural romance with this woman that I loved. It would be so easy.

Why was it then so hard?

Every time I got to the point in my mind where I knew this was the logical next step, my heart sank. When I anticipated the loss I would feel if I ran away, I was overcome. It wasn't that I couldn't give up my new weekly habits or the new friends. I couldn't give up Jesus. Where would I ever find a love like his? Who could ever provide me with the security of his eternal affection? Before, this girl had been my whole world. But I could no longer exchange my soul for that. I needed, I wanted, him instead.

This relationship with Jesus is the bedrock of obedience—a truth that is as plain as day in our Thessalonians passage. Paul contrasts the honor and holiness of the Christian with the passionate lust of "the Gentiles *who do not know God*" (emphasis added). The letter is written to people from Gentile backgrounds: non-Jewish converts to faith in the Jewish Messiah. That is part of why Paul adds the qualifier "who do not know God"—he is contrasting who this congregation is now with who they were before. There was a time when they didn't know God, so they slavishly followed their bodies. But now they *do* know him, and it should make all the difference in the world.

Everyone in our world feels the power of sex and romance. When we say Jesus is better than these things, we're not trying to shrink *them* but to magnify *him*. If we tried to pretend that these good gifts were actually bad, we wouldn't even believe ourselves. I knew that there was physical and emotional pleasure to be had in my old life. But the fact was that what Jesus offered me was simply better. His promises were sweeter, his sustaining love richer.

It is pathetically easy for the church to take good gifts and worship them instead of God. This has happened to us with sex and romance, and yet we act as if it's only the world's problem. *They* chase hook-ups and cohabitation, and we click our tongues. Yet we chase sex and romance too, but we just cover it with a Christian veneer. So we get the pleasure of feeling morally superior as we trot about looking for "the one": that starry-eyed soul-mate spouse who will complete us. How foolish! The only "one" who can complete us is Jesus Christ, the Holy One of Israel. How could an image ever replace the real thing?

Singleness for the Christian testifies to the sufficiency of Christ—to the world and to the church. Of course, all sexually faithful people can communicate the worth and beauty of Jesus in this way—straight or otherwise. But somehow in this cultural moment, there is special potency when that is lived out in the life of a same-sex-attracted believer. Perhaps that is because the Western cultural chorus is shouting ever louder that authenticity is only found in following your flesh. To specifically deny what your body wants is a scandal in our culture. When pursuing your desire for same-gender sex and romance would publicly mark you as a hero—brave and strong—denying it makes you a villain.

Another reason why the witness of same-sex-attracted Christians is so powerful is because it's statistically less likely for us to marry. So deciding to follow Jesus carries up front a very high "risk" of not marrying that fictional perfect spouse and attaining that equally fictional perfect sex life. Christian culture has made the same promises as the world:

"In a culture where pursuing your desire for same-gender romance would mark you as a hero, denying it makes you a villain."

true life and adulthood is found in charming romance and hot sex. Just make sure you put a ring on it. Yes, we know singleness is technically commended in the Scriptures. But we can't shake the urge to pair singles up, feeling concerned if they're single too long. We're uncomfortable with celibacy as a choice, and that choice looms large for the same-sex-attracted Christian.

To choose celibacy, Jesus must be really precious to you. What a chance to testify that he is! What an opportunity to call into question the narrative of salvation-by-romance, and to point to what all love dimly reflects. And not just with your words, but, like an Old Testament prophet, with your life. You only give up something awesome for something even better. I could only give up the pleasures of a girlfriend—even someday a wife—for the more pleasurable embrace of Christ.

And in today's world, that witness of radical self-denial is almost impossible to hide.

————

This calls for an important corollary. Those of us who decided to follow Christ in the midst of our same-sex attraction did so because we saw in the gospel the power of salvation—something worth leaving everything for. But the gospel is not just for Day 1 of our life with Jesus. It is for every day that follows. We won't survive if we replace our connection with Jesus with duty or morals.

Looking back, I'm convinced that I didn't just lose my fight on the train to New York. For the whole semester leading up to that, I had been relying on my flesh and not on the Spirit in my attempts to minister to my ex. Was I trying to prove to myself that now I could do it? Was I trying to earn God's favor? More likely I was trying to have old love and new love at the same time: whitewashing that tomb of old love with the magic word "ministry." I wore the name of Jesus, but I was, in many ways, living like a pagan with Christian hobbies.

Where can we actually find power for obedience? The contrast with the "passion of lust" of those who don't know God in 1 Thessalonians 4:4 is "that each of you know how to control his own body in holiness and honor." At first glance, this can sound just like the worldly striving I was stuck in. But a review of the New Testament leads us to better news.

When we believed Christ, we received the Holy Spirit (Ephesians 1:13-14), and God promises that part of the fruit of the Spirit is self-control (Galatians 5:23). We don't produce self-control through our own willpower or good intentions. We don't create self-control from our sincerity. It is fruit, coming forth from our relationship with God. Jesus promised, "I am the vine; you are the branches. Whoever abides in me and I in him, he it is that bears much fruit, for apart from me you can do nothing" (John 15:5).

If we know God and are known by him, we have access to gaining control of our bodies in holiness and honor. But it will never occur apart from him. Let this truth be a witness in us to the church and the world as well: apart from Jesus, we can do nothing. We are not able to stand against our flesh. But he is. We are like barnacles clinging to a whale—we get nowhere, and no sustenance, without him. Unless we cling to

that mighty host, we die. Naked self-denial is no salvation—
it is only of value as part of throwing ourselves on Jesus. It's
true that every disciple must practice Spirit-dependence,
not self-dependence. But again, the context of our Western
culture—which so easily confuses life-giving self-control with
unhealthy repression—affords same-sex-attracted Christians a
unique opportunity to witness to what is possible when you
are united to Christ.

None of this means we will always feel a warm affection for
Christ. Tender emotions toward him are not the same as relying
on him. Many of us will face dark nights of the soul. The call
to abandon Jesus, from within and without, will deafen us.
We will look utterly foolish—pitiable, contemptible, or both.
Then, most urgently, we must take up the means of grace and
trust that he will prove himself true yet again.

———

For any Christian, to display in your life the worthiness and
sufficiency of Jesus is a service to others. But it's possible for
this to stay safely within what our culture deems acceptable—
namely, "You do you; I'll do me. You like Jesus? Great. I like my
girlfriend. Your life, your choice; my life, my choice."

However, the ministry that same-sex-attracted Christians
have to the church and the world must go beyond this
individualistic stance. The costliness of our obedience to God's
words makes demands on others—they can, and should, find
it unsettling. When people are offended by our obedience, it
is because our culture, both inside and outside the church, has
bought the lie that sex is a merely private matter.

Our 1 Thessalonians passage speaks of an abandoned
truth: sex is social. We've seen Paul specify that holiness is
found negatively in abstaining from sexual immorality, and
positively in gaining control over one's own body. But in
1 Thessalonians 4:6, he spells out a third and equal aspect of

this holiness: "… that no one sin against or take advantage of his brother in this matter."

When we sin sexually, it is never isolated. Sometimes we end up lying about our behavior: concealing it from view and building a double life that rots the community. Other times, we justify what we're doing as not sinful, which is both an outrageous offense against God and a sure path leading others to destruction—not to mention ourselves. It is not for nothing that Jesus declared, "Whoever relaxes one of the least of these commandments and teaches others to do the same will be called least in the kingdom of heaven" (Matthew 5:19). Or, as Paul puts it in 1 Thessalonians 4:6: "The Lord is an avenger in all these things, as we told you beforehand and solemnly warned you."

Paul warns against wronging our siblings in Christ when it comes to sexuality. There is a sickening number of ways to do this. One of the most devastating for same-sex-attracted believers is to spread doubt in God's words around sexuality. *Did God really say…?*

As I walked in Central Park, heavy with transgression, I seriously considered going back to my Christian community and not telling anyone what had happened. Couldn't I just keep it to myself? Surely my ex wouldn't tell. It could be my

"Never have I heard my friend's voice so thick with sadness. She kept repeating to me to just come home, to come back."

little secret. I am so thankful the Spirit did not let me take that route; as much as I wanted to save face, I only felt turmoil about telling that lie.

When we got back to the dorm room, I called Sylvia. She was at a Christmas party. I told her everything through snotty tears. Never before or since have I heard my friend's voice so thick with sadness. She kept repeating to me to just come home, to come back. The train ride to New Haven was an emotional confusion for me. I felt such regret over my actions but also deep relief from having confessed. I was received back with open arms; my friend shared grief at my sin but also forgiveness and restoration. It was exactly what I needed, and it strengthened me to confess to others who needed to know.

Perhaps you're reading this as someone who is hiding sin from your church community, or who has run away from them altogether. Satan would love you to believe that you've gone too far—that there's no coming back from what you've done. But he's lying. So let me say to you what Sylvia said to me: Come back. Come home. Forgiveness and restoration are waiting for you in the arms of Christ.

But there's a word of warning here for those who find themselves on Sylvia's side of the phone call. I can't imagine the distress I would have felt had I confessed my sin and received back a reassurance that what I had done wasn't really so bad. That I could have that life if I just baptized it in Christian colors, called it by Christian names. It would have kicked my knees right out from under me, when I could already barely stand.

As far as I can tell, most people change their minds on this issue out of deep sympathy. Folks hate the historic mistreatment of gay and lesbian people. They hear and misinterpret Jesus's call to judge not. They believe that opening the door for same-sex romance reflects God's love, because they've bought the cultural lie that only in marriage can adulthood and joy be achieved.

People in this frame, who want the best for their neighbors, see the plausibility of what we might call revisionist readings of

Scripture—that is, interpretations of the Bible that conclude that same-sex romance and sex are not wrong, and that Scripture supports monogamous same-sex faithful marriage. Such people have usually been exposed to biblical framing of sexuality that is all about *no*, and not about God's greater *yes* to us in Christ. This leaves them aching for a better vision, and the revisionist view best matches the love songs and movies that speak to them.

It is not hard to go to a Christian bookstore or website and find an empathetic teacher of this position. This is not new. The Bible's words on life and sexuality have offended every culture in every age, as people have risen up to try to save God from his own bad image. What if it's not him who needs saving but us? If God never says anything that contradicts us, if we find ourselves in total alignment with a perfectly righteous all-knowing being who comprehends all mystery, which is more likely: that we're just like him or that we're missing something?

Paul wants to protect God's people from themselves. He says explicitly at the end of our passage, "Therefore whoever disregards this [that is, God's teaching on sexuality], disregards not man but God, who gives his Holy Spirit to you" (1 Thessalonians 4:8).

A crucial ministry of same-sex-attracted Christians is to point to the validity of God's word over our deep feelings. Our costly obedience publicly announces that God's design is more beautiful than our rearrangements. It warns that redefining sin harms all people, not least same-sex-attracted believers. We already face immense pressure from the world; to be questioned by our siblings in Christ only increases the burden. We are a reminder from the Lord to his church that his law is good, and that trying to work around it brings ruin, despite good intentions. We are a testament that it's us who need to be rescued, not the Bible.

———

Our lives and obedience are a warning against taking away from God's good word, and they also warn against adding to it.

Parts of the church have historically been a source of pain and mistreatment for gay and lesbian people, trafficking in stereotypes, cruel jokes, and in some cases physical violence. Even today there are youth who are trying to understand their sexuality in the light of the gospel who are being kicked out of their homes or having their inheritances or money for college held in ransom. Some Christians still flirt with a fixation on understanding what causes these attractions, and with a determination to make people straight.

This is why we need the Bible more than ever. Every person who loves the Scriptures can, like a Pharisee, be prone to add to them. So many Christians over time have felt a deep disgust at homosexuality and a suspicion of gay people. Rarely did they look closely at the Bible to see what the correct response to this would be. Instead, cruelty and turning away were permitted, as if that were the proper outworking of God designing marriage to be between a man and a woman. The Bible was misused, misinterpreted, and quite literally thrown at image-bearers, like the stones meant for the woman caught in adultery.

All people are sexually broken, in need of forgiveness and transformation. We need to believe God: that it's his kindness that leads us to repentance (Romans 2:4). We must be clear about and faithful to what the word says about sexuality—all of it. Which means not placing extra burdens on some while excusing others.

Same-sex-attracted believers have a ministry in the church to show the good news that, even in the face of enduring temptation, life in Christ can be found. That his Spirit provides power for holiness, so that no one in church needs to shrug shoulders and accept the devastation and destruction caused by sexual sin in any of its forms. That all of us, whatever our sexuality, need and deserve the same grace and truth over time.

As I've gotten to know more same-sex-attracted Christians, I've learned that I am in a minority: I never experienced bullying or harm from the hands of Christians because of my attractions. And I never felt quietly sworn to secrecy by the culture around me. Consequently, I didn't face extra barriers when I heard the gospel. I long for all same-sex-attracted people to have such a clear path to Jesus Christ, with only the gospel itself as a stumbling block.

I believe that one of the most beautiful things that faithful same-sex-attracted Christians bring to the church and to the world is this clear path: a vision of Jesus more beautiful than romance, of the Spirit empowering us to live in holiness, and of the Bible not as a death sentence but a balm of hope.

And, as we'll see in the next chapter, the reclamation of Christian siblinghood is another way in which we're called to help the church.

CHAPTER 5

UNEXPECTED RELATIONSHIPS

God absolutely blesses faithful same-sex relationships. Though same-sex marriages are sinful and out of bounds for the Christian, marriage itself is only one type of relationship. God has made each of us for community, and same-sex relationships—namely, friendships and other platonic relationships—are an important part of that. We don't have to look long in the Bible to see that this is true. Ruth and Naomi come to mind—two women bound together in the LORD through hardship, whose commitment to each other sets in motion a chain of events, and continues a family line, which leads to the birth of King David. Or consider that great man himself, who declared that Jonathan's love for him was greater than the love of women (and we know that David certainly had many lovers). Or look to Jesus, who had deep same-sex friendships with John, Peter, and Lazarus, among others.

Likewise, our own experience tells us that same-sex relationships of this kind are powerful and meaningful. As a campus minster, I routinely see that it is in the company of other young women that young women start to flourish in faith.

So God absolutely blesses faithful same-sex relationships. And because he knows our weakness and sin, he gives us in the Scriptures just the instruction and correction we need to cultivate these well. As is often the case, God's words come to us not merely as proclamations but as pictures. The dominant image of healthy same-sex relationships in the Bible, and especially the New Testament, is that of a *family*.

This might give you pause. After all, one of the chief pains for the same-sex-attracted Christian is that they might not get to experience the joys of nuclear family life. And didn't we already spend time critiquing the church's embrace of salvation-by-romance? Family seems to be the one thing denied and also a false hope, all at once.

The confusion comes from having swapped the lesser for the greater. Family is indeed good—it was designed by God to bless us. But when we try to take the small-unit family of biology and legal definition, and have it stand in for the big-unit family of being united in Christ Jesus, we falter. When we are born again, we become brothers and sisters in the church, and it is precisely here that we should experience the richness of same-sex relationships.

I originally set out to write about friendship: specifically, same-sex friendship. I wanted to share how God has used it so powerfully in my life, and how I am convinced that we don't need to be afraid of it but should embrace it wisely. If you've read this far, you've seen that I simply could not have survived without friends.

Yet as I searched the Scriptures, praying and thinking, I realized that the notion of friendship is not robust enough to capture what God wants to do with his community. Nor, I think, is it robust enough to provide what Christians need, including the same-sex-attracted. Though friendship is a biblical and valid concept, it properly belongs underneath the main theme of family. In this way, same-sex-attracted believers are protected and nurtured according to our particular vulnerabilities as well as being able to serve from our particular strengths.

———

But how does this work? To help us get our footing, let's examine a teaching of Jesus on the role of family in the life of the disciple.

It occurs in Mark 10, in the aftermath of Jesus's interaction with the rich young ruler. The ruler wanted to be a disciple—he even claimed to have obeyed pretty much all of the second table of the Ten Commandments. What dedication and sincerity! Yet he was not able to give up his great wealth; it proved to own too much of his heart, and he went away deeply sorrowful.

"And Jesus looked around and said to his disciples, 'How difficult it will be for those who have wealth to enter the kingdom of God!'" (Mark 10:23). This was shocking because in the Jewish mind wealth was seen as a sign of God's favor. Yet in the face of his disciples' amazement, Jesus restated his point. Eventually Peter interjected, looking for recognition that he and the others had given up everything to become disciples. Jesus didn't rebuke him for seeking affirmation, but he responded at length:

> *29 Truly, I say to you, there is no one who has left house or brothers or sisters or mother or father or children or lands, for my sake and for the gospel, 30 who will not receive a hundredfold now in this time, houses and brothers and sisters and mothers and children and lands, with persecutions, and in the age to come eternal life. 31 But many who are first will be last, and the last first. (Mark 10:29-31)*

Notice how seamlessly Jesus moves from discussing wealth in the form of possessions to wealth in the form of relationships.

He had asked the ruler to give up material goods because that was that man's particular hang-up. But for many would-be disciples, the cost has been relationships—arguably a much more significant loss. This is salient for people in the LGBT+ community. To come to Christ is not merely an individual affair; it will fracture deep ties among people who have become so close that they are felt to be family. This is real loss and must be acknowledged.

Before I became a Christian, I wasn't deeply involved in the LGBT+ community—my hometown didn't provide much access to it, and I came to Christ so early at Yale that I didn't get involved with it there. Yet I did lose meaningful relationships, and it hurt. Two of my favorite friends from high school expressed their disgust at my conversion to my face, and never interacted with me again. I can't pretend to know what leaving behind a whole world of people for Jesus would feel like, but I know it is a road many others have walked. If we in the church want to see our neighbors who identify as gay come to faith, we have to understand that this change in relationship and family identity is part of what Jesus will bring, and it is costly.

When Jesus warned about riches, the disciples balked, asking, "Then who can be saved?" (Mark 10:26). We might feel the same about the idea of leaving precious relationships, about having them so altered that they never again provide the same sense of comfort and home that they once did, about potentially being banished from them. We are not crazy to feel this. God made us for community. To weigh the cost of losing LGBT community is to grasp the radical nature of discipleship. Everyone who enters Christ must leave behind the treasures of their former life. Is it even possible for us to make that leap?

"With man it is impossible," Jesus said, "but not with God. For all things are possible with God" (Mark 10:27). This puts its finger on the heart of the matter: only God can work this miracle of salvation. The price will always look too high until God sheds the light of the gospel of the glory of God in the face of Jesus Christ upon the heart of a woman or man. Without the beauty of Jesus, we won't leave the safety of our LGBT family.

So the first reassurance of Jesus is this: though leaving the riches of relationship is humanly impossible, God has made a way.

———

The second reassurance found in this passage is just as precious: we may give up real family to become a disciple, but we are born again into a hundredfold riches of kin. Not in some distant future: right now. We are not orphans—we are adopted into a boisterous clan, a place in which to love and be loved, a family in which to grow.

My first introduction to Christian community was my campus fellowship—Yale Students for Christ, or YSC. I began to bond with these men and women, doing official group events but even more, just spending normal moments with them. Standing in the video rental store Blockbuster for three hours arguing over which 90-minute movie to rent and talk all the way through, for example.

These fellow students taught me the basics of the faith, to be sure. My freshman Bible study in the book of Ephesians was led by Sylvia. But even more, it was watching them that taught me the rhythms of faith. I remember sitting on Sylvia's floor one April day, and another YSC girl called her, distressed about a boy. I heard Sylvia not only give her standard good-friend advice but naturally and easily ask her about how she had been praying through her feelings, and then offer to pray right there with our friend on the phone. These were little things, but they showed me without telling me that discipleship is about every nook and cranny of life.

One of the most helpful things was all the physical affection displayed in the group. My friends overflowed with hugs! And it was common for the women of the group, when hanging out, to show casual physical affection as a form of love. It happened more than once that I fell asleep with my head on a friend's lap.

I was learning by immersion why it made more sense to call these people siblings. The first benefit of the sibling relationship over mere friendship is that it is chaste by default. This is true even though it is an intimate relationship. With

"Sibling relationships in Christ create immense freedom to love."

biological brothers and sisters, there is no suspicion around physical affection, the sharing of secrets, or spending time together, because that group is off-limits for romance. It creates immense freedom to love.

I think this is particularly apt in our age right now, when everyone crows about wanting to marry their best friend. Friendship is a beautiful component of a healthy marriage, but who says it has to be the main criterion? Apparently, social media. Having this strong of a link between friendship and romance does us a disservice. It primes us to see erotic potential, or danger, lurking in every single friendship. Perhaps a reclamation of sibling language more broadly would help us pursue the chasteness meant for that relationship. The church is meant to be a safe place to experience the intimacy and physicality that we all need. Especially for those who are single long term, the church is meant to be where family happens in these particular ways.

Well, you may be thinking, that sounds fine—except for the pesky fact that sexual attraction can and does brew in these happy communities. And you would be right. By no means should the sibling metaphor lead us into spiritual laziness! We know that sexual immorality, like the proverbial hurricane, can begin with the faintest flutter of a butterfly wing. How in the world do we balance our need for, and right to, spiritual family, when the specter of romantic and sexual attraction hangs over us? Even when we look at how the church has handled *male-female* relationships, we don't feel particularly hopeful. There does seem to be much alternating between the ditch of sexual sin and its opposite—an unhealthy avoidance of male-female friendship and partnership altogether.

At first, this wasn't an issue for me. I wasn't romantically or sexually attracted to any of the women of YSC, even though I was deeply attracted to them as friends. And I was understandably not attracted to any of the men. But about a year after I came to Christ, I went on a summer trip with a broader group of students involved in campus ministries, out to Yellowstone National Park. It had been six months since I had ended things with Anna, and I was feeling strong. I was not prepared to meet a fellow Christian on my trip and discover that I was physically and emotionally attracted to her.

I'm so thankful to God that I didn't hide it and try to deal with it on my own. Since I really didn't know what to do, I told the staff woman who was assigned to disciple me all about it. We talked and prayed about what it looks like to recognize attraction but not act on it mentally or physically. We also decided together that I would tell my small group about it so that I would have extra accountability and prayer. There was something about even the simple fact of it being known among my sisters that disempowered the attraction. Sin loves to brew in secret—bringing even the potential for sin to the attention of others helped me nip it in the bud. Eventually, by God's grace, that initial attraction faded, and that sister and I developed a lovely friendship.

But let's be real. Sometimes attraction *is* too strong, and staying close in the friendship is not a healthy option. I've had other situations where I chose to limit my contact with some women for the sake of my purity—no budding friendships there. How in the world are we supposed to tell the difference between what is wise and unwise? Can't there be some handy chart we consult to know what action to take?

This is hard enough when the attraction is physical—a desire to connect sexually. It can become even more confusing when the attraction is romantic. Even the word "romantic" is difficult to pin down a definition for. In our culture, romance is typically involved with the pair-bonding of a couple. It is often intense, emotional, exclusive, and unique—it is usually considered unfaithful to have more than one romantic relationship at a time. As Christians, we should be free to be critical of the idolization of romance as a construct, because it holds a power in our society that is not reflected biblically—more on this is in the next chapter.

But if we embrace romance as Christians, it should only be between spouses, or male-female couples moving strongly in that direction. Romance is not appropriate between people of the same sex, just as it is not appropriate between siblings. Think of the intimacy of healthy sisters. They are close emotionally, often having intimate access to each other's lives. This relationship can be a special blessing, a cherished reality. But it would veer into unhealthiness if one sister was unreasonably jealous of the other having close friendships with anyone else, or if the sisters felt possessive of each other's time or emotions.

Same-sex-attracted Christians must have some same-sex friendships that mirror the best of close siblinghood. But it is all too painfully possible that we can slide into falling in love; probably each of us has experienced this to a greater or lesser extent, and it can be brutal. We should be free to love and enjoy our friends without owning them or being owned by them, or without allowing them to fill all our emotional needs. We're not to pair-bond with our friends and siblings, even as we grow deep relationships. As comedian Mindy Kaling said on her show *The Mindy Project*, a best friend isn't a person; it's a tier.

But let's not throw the baby out with the bathwater. As a same-sex-attracted believer, if I am experiencing healthy platonic intimacy with friends, including appropriate physical affection, I will be better prepared to fight my flesh when illicit romantic and sexual attraction rears its head. Healthy closeness and healthy touch will leave us less vulnerable to sin's deceitful counterfeit offers. Jesus wants us to have family so that we can experience life to the full and be strengthened to fight temptation.

———

So the first benefit of sibling language is that it properly aligns us to what non-marital intimacy is to look like—away from sexual and romantic bonding and toward proper affection and closeness. Another benefit that siblinghood has over friendship is that it is unchosen: that is, we don't pick our family; we simply receive them. Our friends, however, are based more often on choice. The unchosen nature of family is beneficial because it battles against our tendency to separate into affinity groups, or, more concerningly, to pair off and treat best friends like spouses.

It is important to note that it is not wrong to have some siblings that you are closer to than others. And that closeness is friendship. In the novel *Pride and Prejudice* sisters Jane and Elizabeth Bennet share a special bond, a close friendship, within a sibling set. Jesus also seems to have had a special closeness with some of his disciples over others. We humans are communal, and there is so much life to be found in close relationships. The ease and delight when you just "get" someone, and it is mutual, creates a warm experience of home.

These relationships are the context for soul-sharpening, where the "one-anothers" of Scripture are particularly practiced—commands to love one another, encourage, pray for, bear with and even if necessary rebuke one another. A good friend can tell when you're hiding something. They can tell when you're low, sometimes even before you notice. They can call out special giftings that you've been given to serve the body with, and prod you toward fuller faithfulness. Here, there is safety to discuss real fear and struggle, and to offer and receive true help, not platitudes. Close friendship is a treasure.

But as with any powerful gift that God gives us, human sinfulness and weakness can cause us to wield it falsely. How easy it is to spend all our time with the person or the group we prefer, not engaging in full body life. The church family, like

"Close friendship is a treasure. Here there is safety to discuss real fear and struggle, and to offer and receive true help."

every human family, has members that are more difficult to love. It will include individuals who we don't naturally "click" with—maybe even some who get on our very last nerve. It is right here that we are called to love. That doesn't require you to feel the same affection toward all, or that you spend equal amounts of time with all. But functional disconnection can't be love, either.

We are all painful works in progress when it comes to biblical community. But God's placement of us into his family isn't just an optional bonus for extroverts. It's a blessing and a challenge—just what we need to live fully. We need full family, with all its pitfalls and prizes. The larger collection of brothers and sisters can help our close friendships not sink in on themselves like an ingrown toenail of the body. And our close friendships within the body can be special sources of love and blessing, as we team up with those we love best to use our gifts for loving widely. The push and pull of our chosen friendships within the gift of unchosen family provides both safety and challenge, as God's Spirit provides what we need and also lifts our gaze higher.

This is true for all, and no less for those of us who experience same-sex attraction. The broad family is meant to protect us from inwardness too, which is especially helpful given the potential for us to develop romantic feelings for our close friends. Not that we're attracted to *all* people of our same sex—but we know that attraction and intimacy are complicated, and we need to be watchful of temptation. Living our close relationships embedded in broader family is designed to be one tool to help us identify if a friendship is taking on romantic hues, or keeping us from participating well in the local body. Not everybody needs to know your business, but we must develop sibling-life with enough people so that we can get—and provide!—help in time of need.

———

A third benefit of family is its intergenerational nature. Some of us do have older and younger good friends. But it is much more typical in friendship to segregate ourselves by age. If that's our main form of body life, we become spiritually anemic, or like a toddler who refuses anything but his two favorite foods.

Family includes everyone from the elderly down to newborns. Paul famously teaches in Titus 2 about older women teaching the younger ones. We get even more out of this text when we realize we are always older *and* younger than someone! Christianity is not a spectator sport. We're called off the bench, into the action.

Faithful men and women in the decades ahead of us offer special help for those of us with same-sex attraction. They have lived entire lives with sexual bodies. Perhaps they don't experience precisely what we do, and yet they too possess fallen bodies. They too fight indwelling sin. Many of them have probably lived through misplaced romance or fraught friendship. If we lived our closest relationships within the sight of trusted older brothers and sisters, wouldn't we gain great perspective? Perhaps a timely warning, as well as timely encouragement? It was, after all, my friend Anita, who graduated from university when I was not yet three years old, who asked me what I would do if my ex kissed me in Manhattan.

This encouragement and help will be especially valuable for those of us who remain single—a topic we will address more in chapter 7. Our culture gives almost no realistic vision of what that life is like. But perhaps the Lord will provide an older single sibling to help light that way, in dependence on Christ.

Honestly, I long for older brothers and sisters to relate to— my local church situation has mostly been one of drowning in small children while being a desert of anyone over 45. At the same time, even when Anita warned me, I still rushed into sin. I'm not trying to paint intergenerational siblinghood as a cure-all solution. Yet I do believe that in our culture, which worships youth and despises the old, we have a lot to learn from the biblical vision of family. Our fight against sin and for the holiness of Christ is meant to go the distance. We need to follow, and become, faithful guides.

———

While one vulnerability for same-sex-attracted believers is the potential to develop romantic or sexual feelings in our same-gender relationships, a second danger is present as well. That is, our church body may harbor dangerous ideas around sexuality, and so the community experience may not be all that we need it to be.

On one side, we may be in a church that is dangerously lax or even outright disobedient when it comes to biblical sexuality. How can we receive strength for our fight against our temptations if our elders or our siblings think we're crazy for trying? Sin works primarily through deceit. Being exposed constantly to empathetic but biblically unsound teaching will provide just the ear-tickling words our flesh wants to hear. I cannot encourage you to remain in a body that takes your struggle against sin as a false pursuit. A church like this is a dangerous place to be.

On the other side, we may be in a church family that still believes in dangerous things like reparative or conversion therapy—an outworking of the misguided belief that sexual holiness is equated with heterosexuality. Or their position may be hypocritical—winking at pornography or other sexual sins among straight people, while acting as if merely experiencing temptation toward the same sex is itself actual sin. These siblings may spend an inordinate amount of time trying to figure out what causes same-sex attraction, as if we could reverse the effects of the fall through human tactics. Some Christians still consider those who experience same-sex attraction as somehow "less than," or inherently dangerous or untrustworthy.

Negotiating these kinds of church contexts calls for great discernment. In some situations, your presence in a church with some of these flaws could be just what God uses to bring that family into greater alignment with his word. Your life and words may bring them into the realization that many of their assumptions about and stances toward same-sex-attracted people are not biblical. Relating to you as a brother or sister in Christ may be exactly what they need. If this ends up being the case, however, we must watch, lest we develop an inflated sense of our own importance or a myopic focus on this one topic of sanctification.

But there could be a situation that just isn't healthy for you, where you'd spend so much mental and emotional energy in engaging with these difficulties that you would be distracted from the normal rhythms of discipleship and Christian family. These difficulties may even become wounding, especially if you have experienced forms of abuse in the past. We need to be in a family where we will be helped in living the Christian life, no matter which set of temptations we face, but not in a family that zeros in on one set of temptations in a disruptive way. Don't try to navigate this alone—pray for the Lord to provide trustworthy siblings to help you move forward wisely, by his Spirit and his word.

God blesses same-sex relationships that are faithful to Christ, and those relationships are meant to be expressed in faithful brotherhood and sisterhood in Christ. He promised abundant family now to those who leave what the world provides for his sake and his kingdom. He is faithful; he will surely do it. Though we have particular vulnerabilities and needs, God desires for us to experience the richest blessings of family and friendships in his church.

For some of us, that even means marriage.

CHAPTER 6

UNEXPECTED MARRIAGE

In 2007, I married a man. But it wasn't because I had fallen in love.

That idea might surprise you. It surprised me too. After all, I had grown up imagining that one day I would find *that* person—the one who filled up my thoughts like helium, who tripped my body's alarms, a wanted intruder. We would meet *and just know*. Marriage would come as naturally as the passing of time. It would be like the drawn bow that shot us both forward into our futures.

My previous experiences of falling in love had not led to marriage. But I had tasted that delicious reality and knew it was possible to drink it again. The only problem, of course, was that I had always fallen in love with women, and never with a man. I wasn't convinced, based on my attractional history, that *that* was possible.

This left me on uncertain ground as a new Christian in college. Naturally, there was plenty of buzz around potential and real romantic relationships in our fellowship. I, however, didn't really know my place in it all. The prospect of singleness stretching out for decades was real, and I took in that vista as a teenager and wondered: could that be a road I would walk?

It seemed to me that if the core of marriage was romance, and romance with men was not possible for me, then the case was closed.

But what if I had the premise wrong?

———

When I got involved in freshmen Bible study as a new Christian, we were studying the book of Ephesians. Opening the Scriptures together, teasing out the meaning, asking each other tough questions about whether we saw its truths penetrating our daily lives—this was the highlight of my week. We would laugh, think, and explore—a group of young men and women in Christ together.

We went through the book a chunk at a time, which naturally led us after the spring break to Ephesians 5:22-33:

22 Wives, submit to your own husbands, as to the Lord. 23 For the husband is the head of the wife even as Christ is the head of the church, his body, and is himself its Savior. 24 Now as the church submits to Christ, so also wives should submit in everything to their husbands.

25 Husbands, love your wives, as Christ loved the church and gave himself up for her, 26 that he might sanctify her, having cleansed her by the washing of water with the word, 27 so that he might present the church to himself in splendor, without spot or wrinkle or any such thing, that she might be holy and without blemish. 28 In the same way husbands should love their wives as their own bodies. He who loves his wife loves himself. 29 For no one ever hated his own flesh, but nourishes and cherishes it, just as Christ does the church, 30 because we are members of his body. 31 "Therefore a man shall leave his father and mother and hold fast to his wife, and the two shall become one flesh." [32] This mystery is profound, and I am saying that it refers to Christ and the church. [33] However, let each one of you love his wife as himself, and let the wife see that she respects her husband.

I don't remember much of our specific discussion of this passage, but I do remember feeling confronted by it. Our Bible studies took about two hours—as with this chapter, this was not long enough to extract all the sap from Paul's words. Nonetheless, we did walk away agreeing on three basic truths.

First, Paul is clear that marriage is designed to mirror a prior and more prominent relationship: that of Christ and his church. Thus human marriages are good but also not the greatest good. We've covered that idea in depth in chapter 2, but it is important to see the clarity of that in this passage. The purpose of human marriage is bound up with sex difference because the different sexes represent different, non-interchangeable partners in the divine marriage. The husband adopts one posture and the wife another because the fundamental postures of Christ and the church are also different from each other. This makes sense given that Christ and the church have irreducibly different roles to play. The differences in both, however, are meant to combine into an elegant unity. This is why Paul quotes from Genesis, "… and the two shall become one flesh" (v 31).

Second, there are a lot more words to the husband than to the wife—and what words they are! This husband is no passive patriarch receiving service and sandwiches or a tyrant distributing orders from above. No, this husband is a lover, and his love is costly, attentive, and tender. It's a beautiful vision, and a sober one for any man who would consider becoming a husband. It is a call to die, not to reign—which, not surprisingly, sounds a lot like the leadership of the Christ whom these husbands are meant to model.

Third and finally, it was clear to us freshmen that there wasn't any way to skirt around the word "submit" when it came to wives, though it made us squirm. Even so, it was helpful to notice a couple things. For starters, the verse *just before* the call for wives to submit references the mutual submission of all Christians to each other. Submission is not a special call for certain Christians at certain times, but a universal attitude that must be claimed. Additionally, we noted with relief that no one is *making* the wife submit, forcing submission. This is not about one party subjugating another. Instead the wife—with dignity, clarity, and agency—chooses to conduct herself in a certain way, precisely because of her allegiance to Christ. Submission, then, is a spiritual discipline of placing oneself underneath another Christian's rightful authority, using one's gifts to support their leadership.

This submission is never about accepting abuse or being pressured to sin. Because Jesus is her ultimate Lord, a wife has the right to safety and freedom from husbandly harm. As God's people, we must never turn a blind eye to sin and the abuse of power. That fundamentally distorts the individual image-bearing of the man and the woman as well as destroying the picture they are supposed to create together. We know too well how capable fallen humans are of these treacheries.

Together then, we left that Bible study with a vision that felt paradoxical: marriage is about love but not necessarily about romance. Marriage is a picture. It's not that romance necessarily has to be out of the frame. It's just that the love which marriage points to is even richer than that. God has initiated with his people a powerful, triumphant love. A love that seeks and saves, that washes and restores. That stays put, even until the moment of death—a hand held, a gaze met, a promise kept.

Two months into my faith, what did I truly know of that?

———

Andrew and I met in a living room in Dover, New Hampshire, more than a year later. We had both been accepted for the same summer missions project in Yellowstone National Park, and I was joining a caravan of mostly University of New Hampshire students on the long drive to Wyoming. Up until that point, I had only spent time with my Yale Christian friends. Being around the boisterous UNH students caused me to turtle in, hiding behind a copy of *The New Yorker* on a couch.

A pale, skinny boy didn't want me to stay hidden though. Andrew drew me out, not into the whole crowd but at least into conversation with him. As the pack of us journeyed

"It was clear to me that Andrew was a good kind of friend. But it never occurred to me to be interested in him romantically."

west, camping and devouring fast food and blasting out bad Christian music, friendships began to knit. It was clear to me that Andrew was a good kind of friend. But it never occurred to me to be interested in him romantically.

As the summer came to an end and I transitioned to the beginning of my junior fall, Andrew sent me a message on AIM (or AOL Instant Messenger, which is what we used in the sad world before WhatsApp and iMessage existed).

A: hey! what's up?

R: hold on…

And I never did get back to him. The next time we communicated at all was also initiated by him, three months later. It was the day I took the train ride home from New York

City, in turmoil over my disobedience with my ex-girlfriend. Andrew called me out of the blue. He was on duty as a resident's assistant in the honors dorm at the University of New Hampshire. He was meant to be looking out for other students and enforcing university rules, but honors students never caused a ruckus, and I came to his mind during his uneventful shift. He was wondering how I was doing and how he could pray for me. Because he had known my full story from the summer, and because he was such a trustworthy and sympathetic guy, I told him everything. I remember how helpful it felt to talk to him, and how grace-filled and encouraging he was to me as a brother.

Under a month later, he and I were both at the Boston Winter Conference, an event put on to encourage college students in their Christian faith, and to invite those who don't follow Jesus to do so. I was in a strange place in the aftermath of my sin, and one that felt to be dripping with danger. I had never been more intellectually convinced that I was completely forgiven by Christ. Yet I also felt no emotional response to this fact. My heart was a heavy, dead thing. I went in to that conference asking the Lord to help me.

In his mercy, he heard my prayer. The conference was bursting with gospel truth, and my heart began to thaw. I was reassured that God isn't just good in abstract, like a definition in a dictionary put out of sight. He was good *to me*, for me. Forgiveness was not a judicial act alone but the lingering hug of a family member, a restitution and repetition of love. Like Peter, I was being restored after a ghastly offense against Jesus, the One who loves me.

It was a seminal moment in my young Christian life. And right in the middle of it, Andrew started lightly—could it actually be?—flirting with me. I could barely handle it.

I wasn't interested in Andrew *like that*. I was hoping that I was reading the signals wrong, even after he asked me to breakfast alone on the last morning of the conference. But a day later, back at our respective campuses, he called me again, asking if he could make the three-and-a-half-hour drive down to New Haven to see me. I didn't feel that I could say no, but I also panicked. I distinctly remember cuddling up with Sylvia as I told her about it and squealing, "I don't want to date Andrew Gilson!"

———

Perhaps my initial reluctance reminds you of bad things you've heard about marriages like mine, between a same-sex-attracted believer and a member of the opposite sex. This is all so culturally loaded that I confess I feel the danger of telling you the truth about my initial hesitancy. In the winter of 2006, I knew exactly nothing about "ex-gay" ministries like Exodus International. I was born too late and not into a church. Even when I came to faith, there was never mention of groups like these.

Not everyone had it so easy. In some corners of Christendom, especially in the 1980s and 90s, there was pressure on same-sex-attracted people to achieve heterosexuality. Freedom from these desires was held up as the sign that God was at work and that bondage was broken. But, as we covered in chapter 3, holiness does not equal heterosexuality. God is just as much at work in those of us who pitch daily battle against same-sex lust as in any who have that temptation removed. It is the privilege of the child of God to be removed from the guilt of sin, but we do not yet enjoy the removal of temptation.

It is not surprising, however, that a consequence of the idolization of heterosexuality was the pressure for same-sex-attracted Christians to enter in to marriages. I'm no sociologist, nor have I studied this movement in depth. But I *have* received emails from strangers, brothers and sisters, desperately seeking help: men and women who were promised, implicitly and explicitly, that marriage to a person of the other sex would be the ticket. But to what destination?

The two narratives I've heard the most are that getting married would make a person straight and that getting married would prove—to self and to community—that the same-sex-attracted believer was truly committed to following Christ. These stories make more sense when set in the context of broader attitudes towards sex and marriage in a section of Christian culture at the time. A generation of young people growing up in the church were sold the vision that their reward for saying no to sex before marriage would be a perfect spouse who would provide them with perfect sex until the end of their days.

Where did that leave sincere Christians who grew up experiencing unremitting attraction exclusively to people of their same gender? If you were told on the one hand that the prize for faithfulness to Christ is marriage, but you knew on the other hand that marriage was not an option for you no matter how faithful you were, what then? If the main blessing God had to offer was something that made you shudder to think of it, what were your options? One option was despair. Another option was to desperately try to change your attractions. Other people had decided that that vision was true, and so it must mean that God wanted the same-sex-attracted believer to get married whatever their attractions. Finally, some thought the vision was dreadful and left the church altogether.

The vision of human marriage as the reward for faithfulness to Christ is a deadly lie. Nowhere in Scripture is earthly marriage promised to any of us. Not only is it not promised but it's not even presented as the preferred state of being. Instead, under the new covenant we see that the unmarried and the married have equal dignity and opportunity to image and serve the Lord. They are both beautiful, and both circumstances require the death to self which is at the heart of following Jesus.

Marriage is not promised or preferred. It can't make you straight nor prove that you're committed. It's not the prize for faithfulness, nor the source. Jesus Christ is the prize. The Holy Spirit is the source. God is our Father, our husband, our friend.

We can't pretend that the pressure to marry for same-sex-attracted people in the church is confined to the past. It can still exist today. It can come from inside of you just as easily as

"Marriage is not the prize for faithfulness, nor the source. Jesus is the prize. The Spirit is the source."

from outside. I want to encourage you: whatever your marital state, you are valuable to God and deeply loved. If you're considering marriage, gather safe people who can help you process why. Examine your motives and ask hard questions of your heart. Are you motivated by something not present in the word? It's better to be fully honest before a solemn promise is made before the Lord and his people. There is no shame in clear-sighted evaluation.

But what if you're already in a marriage? What if your story is one of broken promises—to you, by you? There are many stories of people who hoped for change and didn't find it. I've received confessions from spouses who are suffocating under their loneliness or their lack of desire. The secret suspicion that they may have made a mistake catches in their throat. Some have lived like this for years, with promising stretches of married life far outbalanced by longer times of despair.

There is no easy answer in this situation. Sadness, even deep sadness, does not permit sin, which can promise all the joy you want but will never fully deliver. But saying "don't sin" doesn't mean that there is a universally appropriate next step for people found in unhappy marriages. We need the Spirit, the word, and mature Christians to guide us forward. Have we been completely honest with ourselves and with our spouses? Should we consider counseling—individually and as a couple? Where does the gospel need to bear its fruit in this situation?

If you're in that position, friend, you can't move forward alone. You need to seek help and support, today. If you're in the position to be a helper—don't give cheap answers. Yes, the Lord hates divorce. And sin. He is also close to the broken-hearted and carries the burdens of the weary. We're called to participate in that as well. The culture of unbiblical promises about marriage was created corporately, and together we need to attend to those who have been harmed by them.

But it's not enough to tend to the wreckage. Especially if we have any measure of spiritual authority or influence, we need to repair the road that is leading to these accidents. We need to go back to what the Scriptures say on the subject of marriage for all our people, and for our same-sex-attracted people no less. Part of that means teaching that marriage doesn't exist to make people straight, nor is it a means by which to gain spiritual points. It is not promised, and it is not preferable.

But it *is* possible.

———

I had a sense, which I interpreted as the leading of the Spirit, that I should say yes to dating Andrew. Not because I thought it would go anywhere but because I felt that the Lord was asking me to trust him. It was a sense so strong that I couldn't shake it—in fact, in my whole Christian life, I don't know that I've ever had a season when the Spirit of the Lord felt so near to me as in that second semester of my junior year. I've often wondered if that was to save me from running away.

Because Andrew and I lived apart, the majority of our time spent "dating" looked exactly like intentional friendship. We would have chats on the phone about our days and about our spiritual and social lives. He would visit and we'd eat together and hang out with my friends. If there is anything true about Andrew Gilson it is this: he is a good and loyal friend. My affection for him grew very naturally.

By the early summer, I was growing in my suspicion that I would end up married to Andrew.

On the one hand, I truly felt my heart opening and warming to him. He was a kind man with a natural safety. It was easy to have conversations with him about all kinds of things. Especially attractive was that his faith in Jesus Christ was at the very center of his life. There was not a decision that he made that didn't flow from the fountain of his personal faith. Not only that but he also felt called to go into full-time college ministry, as did I.

On the other hand, the relationship seemed deficient in two areas that had been of vital importance in my other main romances. The first was the centrality of big ideas. That's not to say that Andrew wasn't a thinker—he was just not drawn to the academic and the esoteric as I am. He'd rather take something apart and put it back together or listen to a biblically faithful and pastorally encouraging sermon than read a textbook with more footnotes than text. It was jarring to experience that while he and I had plenty of things to share, when it came to certain types of ideas, he was willing to talk, but they didn't light him up in the same way. Did that mean we were incompatible? Hadn't that always been a deep source of romantic spark for me?

The second lack was what I would describe as intense attraction. With my high-school girlfriend and with Anna,

I felt an emotional and sexual pull that seemed right out of songs and movies. It felt as unstoppable as a tidal wave, as appealing as smelling a feast from the next room. My stomach would physically churn, my heart would catch in my throat— at times I could ache with longing. It was sexual, yes, but it was also more than that.

How could I describe what I felt toward Andrew? Whereas the other feeling was overpowering and explosive, the feeling in me that was growing toward him felt much more vulnerable—like a small flame being protected by cupped hands from the wind. I couldn't deny that it was real, yet I worried whether something like that could possibly fuel a marriage. Nothing in my cultural playbook supported that hypothesis, and nothing in my personal history did either.

This small flame gave me moments of panic that following summer. Yet I continued to feel the presence of the Lord, sensing that he wanted me to stay. I couldn't have made it through that time on these feelings alone, however. With a couple of friends, I had hours of conversation about the nature of romance, how much attraction counted as "enough," and what it even meant to be married. In these conversations, I was driven back again to Ephesians 5.

I remembered the lessons I'd gleaned from the passage two years before: that marriage is about love but not necessarily

> "Marriage is about love but not necessarily about romance. It is a covenant designed to tell the story of *the* covenant."

about romance. It is a covenant designed to tell the story of *the* covenant. Faithful, because God's love is faithful. Sexual, because God's love is full of desire and pleasure and closeness. Fruitful, because God's love produces new life. Male and female, because God's love in Christ is one "actor," and his people, the church, are another—and they combine into an elegant unity.

The intense passion that we call romance could certainly be present with all these things. Yet marriage is a bond that can't be fueled on romance alone. Romance bursts bright, but can it burn long? Marriage is not a weekend project, staining the deck. Marriage is a lifelong pursuit, like the construction of a cathedral, which, while sustained by joy, must also weather tears, injury and pain. It must keep being built when joy is hiding away.

I am persuaded that most people in the church have a vision of marriage as the consummation of romance, inseparable from it. This is why so many of us tend to end our marriages when the romance sputters. Too many decisions to marry are not calculated with everything in mind, because romance is present and strong. It reminds me of Jesus's words in Luke 14:28: "Which of you, desiring to build a tower, does not first sit down and count the cost, whether he has enough to complete it?"

Anything of major cost and value requires serious forethought. Marriage shouldn't be entered into on the grounds of passion alone because it is more serious than that. As I processed this in my own dating relationship with Andrew, I ultimately felt freed. Though the relationship started in anguish because of my cultural assumptions and previous experiences, it was such a gift. I didn't need passionate romance per se, but I needed to consider whether I could build a life with this man that displayed Jesus Christ and his church.

Our friendship was solid and growing, and our Christian convictions were completely in line. I discovered that while

Andrew didn't fawn over certain types of big ideas, his life was consumed by the one Big Idea, and this was stabilizing for me. It was easy to see that he would make a great husband and father, and my affections grew. I couldn't prove it scientifically on a scale, but I sensed that I had enough attraction to make it work. And most importantly for me personally, I had a strong sense which seemed to be from the Lord that I should marry Andrew.

I almost wish that weren't true, because I don't want to communicate that I think an impression from God is required to get married, nor even that it is the normal way that he works. But I can't pretend it wasn't a major factor in my decision—a decision I've never regretted.

I didn't marry because I fell in love. I didn't marry to make myself straight, or to prove that I believed in God's sexual ethic. I didn't marry because I was pressured into it externally or internally. I married in hope in and obedience to my Savior, and, yes, with joyful affection toward Andrew.

Marriage is beautiful and possible for same-sex-attracted people, as long as it is entered into with clarity and freedom. It will be where God leads some of his people, perhaps unexpectedly. We'll get a chance to consider more what marriages like these look like practically later on. But just as beautiful and possible is the life dedicated to God in singleness, to which we turn next.

CHAPTER 7

UNEXPECTED CELIBACY

One of the greatest deceptions of the modern West is the idea that you are not truly happy—or even truly alive—until you've found your soulmate.

You'd think a culture drowning in unfaithfulness and casual sex wouldn't be so naive. And yet, something in the impulse is real enough to continue to persuade.

This image of an everlasting romantic and sexual pairing exerts such power over us—even in the face of dramatic, repeated failure—precisely because it hooks into that story that God designed marriage to tell. That story is the gospel: that God saves sinners, so that he might be united to us forever, passionately, fruitfully. So we are right to hold the marriage bed in honor (Hebrews 13:4); it is a great gift.

But it is not the only gift. It is not the only environment in which we can flourish. It is not the only means through which we can seek and declare the kingdom of God. The single, unmarried life has a dignity and a purpose that blesses not only the person but the whole church and culture. In chapter 4 we saw the unique ministry of faithful same-sex-attracted Christians. Sometimes this is played out in the context of opposite-sex marriage, but more often, and more prominently, it happens in the context of singleness. Our faithfulness in singleness deeply challenges the idol that marriage and family have become in the church. It also poses a shocking witness to those outside of it. Clearly the Jesus-centered single life has power and purpose.

Except sometimes—perhaps even much of the time—it just doesn't feel that way.

It would be naive to speak only about the positives of singleness. But we don't want to be dreary about it either, since it is an honorable and good way to live. So how do we communicate accurately about both the ups *and* the downs of singleness? Better yet, how do we live through them, and support others through them?

———

Of all the things in this book, this chapter is the one I feel most self-conscious about. I got married at 22; what in the world do I know practically about singleness?! And yet, right in God's word, it is actively commended. The apostle Paul, a single man himself, recommends it as a way of life in 1 Corinthians 7:8: "To the unmarried and the widows I say that it is good for them to remain single, as I am." I may not have the personal experience to confirm it, but I know God doesn't lie.

But that's the last we'll see of 1 Corinthians 7 in this chapter. Instead, we're going to hear from the Old Testament prophet Isaiah—a man who foretold future judgment for God's people but also future comfort. Tucked into the gathered armfuls of good promises in his book come these words:

> *And let not the eunuch say,*
>   *"Behold, I am a dry tree."*
> *For thus says the* LORD:
> *"To the eunuchs who keep my Sabbaths,*

who choose the things that please me
and hold fast my covenant,
I will give in my house and within my walls
a monument and a name
better than sons and daughters;
I will give them an everlasting name that shall not be cut
off." (Isaiah 56:3b-5)

The verses surrounding this passage mention another social outsider—the foreigner. But we're going to double click on the eunuch. The word translated as "eunuch" was used generally in the Bible to mean a high official in a court, but it was also used for a male who had experienced castration. The second was often the qualification for the first—such a man was not perceived as a sexual threat to the king's harem, for example.

This image doesn't immediately strike us as relatable; few of us have experienced castration or harem guard duty. But perhaps we hear an echo of ourselves in the eunuch's complaint before God: "Behold, I am a dry tree."

There is no sap of life in this man, due to the castration. One of the greatest signs of the blessing and favor of God in the Israelite mind was family. It was a basic duty of Jewish men to find wives and produce offspring in fulfillment of the promise to Abraham. This is how their names would stay alive in Israel. This is how they would know that God was with them. But not so the eunuch. No one would ever marry him; no one would ever call out to him, "Abba! Daddy!"

In a world built for marriage and family, the eunuch was excluded, through no fault of his own. It wasn't merely social exclusion but theological—the very blessings of God seemed connected to marriage and family, like muscle to tendon. The eunuch wasn't part of that living system. He was like a stick on the ground, not a tree rooted in fertile soil.

Like the eunuch in Isaiah's time, for many same-sex-attracted people, the good gift of marriage is simply not an option. Sexual expression is a healthy and important aspect of marriage, which some people would not be able to maintain with an opposite-sex partner, unless God gave them a specific call and specific equipping. That would mean no biological children either.

And it's not just an ache for children. While some people feel called to and content in singleness much of the time, others long for marriage. Some have turned down or left same-sex partners whom they loved deeply in order to follow Christ. They face the pain of knowing they *could* have a romantic and sexual partnership but only by putting away God's blessing. Others have never had a same-sex relationship, and imagining what that might be like, knowing it will never be, can be haunting.

My friend Ed, who is a pastor in Bristol, England, has experienced exclusive same-sex attraction since his teenage years, though he didn't come out until 2013. Now in his 40s, and having been a Christian from a young age, Ed is single because he believes God says "no" to same-sex sexual relationships. In his walk with Christ, he has experienced both the ups and the downs of single life.

While the ache for parenthood is sometimes depicted as a strongly female trait, Ed says that he experiences a deep longing for fatherhood. He told me about one very normal situation where he was gathered with friends, and the discussion turned toward their children—how the kids took after their parents, looked like them or acted like them, for good or for ill. Ed was surprised, given how common these kinds of conversations are, by how deeply his heart throbbed with pain as they all chatted. He would never look at a child and see his own face look back at him. He would never have an heir to teach and pass down a legacy to.

For days and weeks after the incident, his mind would sprint back toward that moment and linger on the lack. Ed had to stare in the face the fact that the spouse-and-two-kids life would not be his, despite his longing.

How similar this is to the eunuch's anguished complaint that he is a dry tree; he has no future and no present. But listen again to how God responds:

> For thus says the LORD:
> "To the eunuchs who keep my Sabbaths,
>   who choose the things that please me
>   and hold fast my covenant,
> I will give in my house and within my walls
>   a monument and a name
>   better than sons and daughters;
> I will give them an everlasting name that shall not be cut
> off." (Isaiah 56:4-5)

The first section of the reply from God marks off which eunuchs he is speaking to. The simple state of being a eunuch doesn't earn blessing from the LORD. But the one whose life is overflowing into obedience demonstrates his love for God, which will not go unseen.

To be clear: our God does not wait for us to show obedience so that we can bribe him into blessing us. That is not the gospel. No, our obedience is the natural and obvious response to a God who is gracious: a way of saying we choose to find our rest and hope in him, and not in anything else.

But obedience will never lead us away from God's blessing—it will always lead us toward it. That's true even when it doesn't look that way in the world's eyes. Consider the particular area of obedience that God picks up on here. Keeping the Sabbath is hard in any culture, because we are fearful of the future and addicted to work. Abstaining from work communicates a trust in the living God for provision and worth. So the eunuch whom God is addressing is a man who is committed to the LORD, as demonstrated by his willingness to keep the Sabbath.

Same-sex-attracted Christians today who are choosing God over sex and romance mirror the eunuch's costly obedience and trust. Certainly it is not *only* same-sex-attracted Christians who do this—all Christians are called to God's high sexual standard. But in this cultural moment, which urges people to boldly take up their LGBT+ identity, those who choose God over sex and romance echo that cry of Peter to Jesus: *Where else would we go? You alone have the words of life.* In a moment when everyone else was walking away, Peter recognized that Jesus had the only thing worth having—all other options were no options at all (John 6:60-69).

And how does God respond to a cry of faith like this? He sees. He knows. As to the eunuch, God promises a heart that draws near to him he will draw near to in return. If you are

> **"If you are choosing singleness because you are clinging to Jesus, it will not go unnoticed by him. Nor will it go unblessed."**

in this position—choosing singleness despite your attractions, despite our culture, because you are clinging to Jesus Christ— it will not go unnoticed by him.

Nor will it go unblessed. The LORD promises this eunuch, this person, two things: a monument and a name. Importantly, they are located "in my house and within my walls" (Isaiah 56:5).

A monument is an object of honor, rooted in a meaningful location. By setting up the monument in his own house, God is declaring that he is irrevocably making the eunuch a part of the family—despite the eunuch's inability to have his own. The same is true of the name, which is mentioned twice in verse 5. Traditionally in our culture, when a woman marries a man, she takes his name, to signify the new family she is helping to create. The marriage relationship confers a new name, in the form of a title: husband or wife. In producing children not only people but names are multiplied—those the parents give to their children, and the names the children create for their parents: Mom and Dad.

These are good names, beautiful. But they are temporary. God declares that to be established in *his* family—the family which all others point to—is to be given a better name. God looks into the eyes of the eunuch and sees the fear: of loneliness, of obscurity, of being utterly cut off—as if it never mattered that that person even existed. To all of these fears, God shouts NO. He answers these fears with a forever family.

God looks at the eunuch *as a eunuch* and promises relationship, exchanging shame for honor. The eunuch doesn't have to pretend he's something else. There's certainly no changing him—castration cannot be undone. Yet he is by no means invisible. To be given a name demands that he be addressed, recognized. And all of these honors and this security will never "be cut off"; they will never come to an end. A physical monument may crumble; a family name may die out. The honor God establishes for this eunuch is everlasting.

To be single and same-sex-attracted in the church has often been an experience of shame, of hiding, of loneliness, of being without family. Constantly fielding well-intentioned questions about why you aren't married or dating. Constantly dodging the ever-present threat of falling in love with a friend while just trying to follow the Lord. Constantly checking to see if you come off "straight enough," whatever that means in your context. Constantly wondering if you'll be invited somewhere Christmas, or even for just a simple night in.

God sees you, and he looks at you with full love. He knows your specific temptations, your specific strengths. He doesn't demand that your personality be subsumed into any cookie-cutter template. He equips you to fight temptation and sin, to serve the body in love and to be loved in return. He gives you his Spirit, not holding back, because he wants you to thrive, not to feebly cross some finish line into death. These promises last forever and they are designed to begin even now.

You are not alone. The eunuch would have felt among the least in the time of the old covenant—the incomplete, the forgotten. But God saw him and called him in his singleness. God sees you and calls you in your singleness.

With that in mind, what do you need to thrive as a single, same-sex-attracted person in a predominantly married, opposite-sex-attracted church? At least three things: a thick relationship with Jesus, life-giving companions, and a realistic, hopeful view of singleness.

———

It has to be acknowledged that there is vulnerability in singleness. No one in your community is obligated to stay in the place where you live, for instance. Job offers, family crises, and other events all too soon pull friends to different towns.

I lived for twelve years in a town with a highly transient population; it was painful and tiring to be constantly left. Deep friendships altered. The energy to invest in new ones faded. Through all that, though, I had my husband. We were never destitute of friends, but having a stable, deep relationship with him was a well I could constantly draw from. If you're a single person in the same position, perhaps you feel at a loss—holding a bucket but not able to consistently find water.

It's true you *need* other humans. But even more than this, you need Jesus. One of his key promises is that he will never leave you nor forsake you. There's not a place you can go to in which his love and presence aren't there. No job calls him away; no more important family member exists.

We know that that's true, and yet it's not always easy to believe. There will be times when, because Jesus is not physically present, you will doubt him. We are not yet in that blessed time to come when we will behold him with our own

"Jesus will never leave you nor forsake you. No job calls him away; no more important family member exists."

eyes. We live now by faith. Singleness will present specific tests of your love of Christ (just as marriage does). Knowing this, you must cultivate your love for him. Not just your knowledge or your service, but your love.

How do we do that? Find out what most stirs your heart for Jesus and invest there. Perhaps it's early mornings with coffee and commentaries, digging deeply into the word. Maybe it's prayer walks with friends, or engaging your heart through service or musical worship. No matter what, take the normal means of grace dead seriously; pursue prayer, Scripture, and acts of mercy as you do air, water, and food.

You will need a thick, durable relationship with Jesus not just because he's the only One who has guaranteed to never leave you—he's also the only One who has guaranteed to never misunderstand you. Sadly, the church's attitude toward same-sex-attracted people can still be one of hostility, suspicion, aggression or exclusion. You may be in community with well-intentioned Christians who say and assume things about same-sex-attracted people that are offensive or painful. In some seasons, perhaps it seems that *only* Jesus gets you. And wonderfully, he always will. He knows your heart, both the evil and the good. He believes no false words of you, while knowing the worst of you. He chose you; he loves you.

———

Jesus must be your foundation. You are made for him—and also made for others. Every human needs friends and people as close as family. But perhaps you're already well aware of your need. Agreeing theoretically doesn't always prepare us for the reality of making and keeping friends: it's hard work.

Every January thousands of people commit to a good diet and exercise. They know it's the right choice for their bodies, and the thought of looking decent come warmer weather is appealing too. Even so, very few make it to February still hitting the weights. It's not that they don't want the *benefits*. It's just so much work!

Having friends in adulthood can feel even more challenging than a regular workout routine. Jesus's most underrated miracle may have been having twelve friends in his early thirties! But the fact that he did make sure to keep others close is certainly instructive. His friends were fickle, sometimes foolish, and even abandoned him in the end. But he cultivated these relationships anyway. For your own sake, and for the sake of those who need your love and personality, persevere in friendship.

Yes, there is the danger that you may fall for a friend. This is again why a close relationship with Jesus is key, so that you can process those feelings in healthy, pure ways. It is also why you should seek not just one deep friendship but do your best to be known broadly. That doesn't mean every friendship needs to be at the same level. It does mean seeking to have more than one safe Christian sibling to know and be known by. This is true for all believers, not least for us who are same-sex attracted. But for those who are unmarried as same-sex-attracted Christians, it is a must.

These broad and deep relationships are the context in which we are meant to live out one of the repeated themes of the New Testament letters: sharing sorrow and triumph with others. The Bible is filled with "one anothers": ways in which our faith is to be exercised with humans who are actually close enough to rebuke us, close enough to hold us when we cry, close enough to buy us the too-expensive gift for our birthday—and vice versa. We need to be close enough to offend and yet be forgiven. To be annoyed and yet persevere in love. How painful that many singles have attempted this in the body and have been rebuffed. If we married people will not seek friendship and family with singles, don't we bear some responsibility when those siblings retreat into isolation or bitterness?

My friend Ed reminded me that even when we are experiencing goodness and life in our friendships, there always lurks the temptation to ask of one friend too much. After all, it's a vulnerability of singleness that you don't have a "default" person, as he calls it—the person you immediately go to for practical help and to process things emotionally. While there's an opposite vulnerability in marriage (to stick exclusively to your spouse for friendship and not pursue broader community), that doesn't shake the single person's lingering belief or secret longing: that you could find that one friend out there to be *your person*.

Ed pointed to a quote from J.C. Ryle that has helped him enormously when he has faced that temptation:

"The Lord Jesus goes with his friends wherever they go. There is no possible separation between him and those whom he loves.

There is no place or position on earth, or under the earth, that can divide them from the great Friend of their souls. When the path of duty calls them far away from home, he is their companion; when they pass through the fire and water of fierce tribulation, he is with them; when they lie down on the bed of sickness, he stands by them and makes their trouble work for good; when they go down the valley of the shadow of death, and friends and relatives stand still and can go no further, he goes by their side. When they wake up in the unknown world of Paradise, they are still with him; when they rise with a new body at the judgment day, they will not be alone. He will own them for his friends, and say, 'They are mine: deliver them and let them go free.' He will make good his own words: 'I am with you always, even unto the end of the world' (Matthew 28:20)." (J.C. Ryle, Practical Religion, p 348)

As Ed put it, you really do have a friend to be your person. He exists; you just haven't fully been in his presence yet. And until that day, our friends now, in depth and breadth, are representatives in part of what Jesus is in perfection—the Friend who never leaves, who always loves, who never fails.

Finally, to thrive in singleness, you'll need a realistic and hopeful understanding of God's vision for the unmarried life.

In Matthew 19 we encounter a very realistic Jesus. He is approached by some Pharisees who try to drag him into a very contentious debate of the time: on what grounds could a man divorce his wife? Jesus's response is pure fire. He rebukes them for sanctioning divorce at all, revealing an extremely high view of marriage—and in his explanation he goes out of his way to affirm that marriage is, by definition, between male and female, which he didn't have to do because that was assumed to be true by his audience.

You can almost feel his disciples squirming under Jesus's strict protection of marriage in general and of women in particular. In verse 10, they reply, "If such is the case of a man with his wife, it is better not to marry." Singleness in this culture was not normal, nor considered blessed. So when they suggest that it's better not to marry, they are almost testing Jesus. Can he be serious in his strict views of marriage, given the alternative?

"But [Jesus] said to them, 'Not everyone can receive this saying, but only those to whom it is given'" (v 11). Jesus acknowledges that singleness can be difficult to receive. He's realistic about it! He's not trying to sell the single life as a song and dance, or brushing aside the weight of it. After all, he is walking through it. He knows and sees.

His next statement in verse 12 brings back the image of our beloved eunuch: "For there are eunuchs who have been so from birth, and there are eunuchs who have been made eunuchs by men, and there are eunuchs who have made themselves eunuchs for the sake of the kingdom of heaven. Let the one who is able to receive this receive it." In the broader context, these eunuchs stand for different types of the unmarried life. Essentially, Jesus acknowledges that you can be in that position for reasons unchosen and chosen—not everyone's situation is the same. So he's realistic, but hope-filled: singleness can be good for the sake of the kingdom of heaven.

Jesus honors marriage while also challenging the demand for marriage. Marriage is not necessary for life like food and water. It is not so central to an individual's flourishing that those who would tamper with it have the right to do so—either by quick divorce, as in the Pharisees' case, or by rejecting its required sexual difference, as in our day. If we can't accept God's vision for marriage, there is an honorable alternative: singleness. It shouldn't be despised, even if that sits uneasily on the ears.

You don't have to pretend that singleness is all roses. Clearly every type of life is touched by the fall and sin, singleness included. You are free to acknowledge its hard edges. Find people who can talk honestly and helpfully about these places of disappointment. Jesus doesn't demand that you grin and bear it.

He also doesn't ask you to wallow in the disappointments of singleness. And sometimes, he'll bless you with a glimpse of what he's doing through it.

Not long ago, Ed was chatting with a fellow minister who said to him, "Hey, I met someone recently whom you discipled." As a pastor, Ed gets to mentor plenty of people, but he was curious to know how this man knew that the guy he'd met had been one of Ed's disciples.

"Oh, that's simple," his friend replied. "He was *just* like you."

Suddenly, the memory of that painful conversation about children came rushing back to him. Except this time, it was accompanied by the realization that he *does* have children. He is passing on his spiritual DNA, producing sons who will live forever. The Lord has not made him a dry tree. Ed is part of a long chain of fruitfulness, as tall as any biological tree and more verdant besides. In fact, as a single man not devoted to wife and natural children, he has the freedom to invest in many more sons than he would otherwise.

In that lovely moment he could taste the blessing; he could feel the peace. This was not some flimsy consolation prize that denied the times of pain and loneliness. This was something from God himself: a monument and a name within God's house.

CHAPTER 8

UNEXPECTED BLESSING

Perhaps you read the previous chapter about my dating and marrying Andrew with a different kind of personal interest—as someone who is straight but is in a relationship or considering a relationship with someone who experiences same-sex attraction. What does it feel like—or what ought it look like—to be on the other side of the table? Can it work? Does it work? Will it work?

In one sense, a relationship like this feels like any normal romantic relationship—the excitement of enjoying this person and being enjoyed in return, the rush of wondering where this is going. You genuinely like them, think about them when they're gone, and laugh even when their jokes aren't funny.

But if you're an opposite-sex-attracted person dating some who is same-sex-attracted, you can also pause in worry that maybe it's all *not* as normal as it seems. Your feelings of affection, desire, and hope are growing—are theirs? Sure, your significant other seems to be interested now, but will it fade? Are you two setting yourselves up for disappointment, by embarking on something foolish in the long run because you're blinded by what's immediate?

Some friends who ask me these questions do so with shame or embarrassment. They're not trying to suggest that they're suspicious of their boyfriend or girlfriend! They don't want to be that person who doesn't really trust same-sex-attracted people. But they're struggling to know where to go for advice—it's hard to find examples of people who have traveled this path. Among the many stories of shipwreck and rough seas, is there any smooth sailing to be found?

To want to walk in wisdom like this is not a betrayal; it is a deep kind of love.

———

My friends Brodie and Greg had known each other for years before Greg asked Brodie out. There aren't too many evangelical Christians in New England, where we all lived. Especially when you both work in ministry, you get to know your circles quickly. Brodie had been single for a while and longed to be married, but Greg had never come on her radar in that way. When he asked her out, she wasn't immediately excited but decided that it wasn't fair not to give him a chance.

Things were going better than she had hoped—they grew closer, and her respect and enjoyment of Greg expanded like lungs filling with air. Around three months in, Brodie started to pray that their dating wouldn't just be about fun times but that they would truly have a chance to speak the gospel to each other, to be an encouragement to one another in Jesus. God answered that prayer in a surprising way: Greg confided in Brodie that he experienced same-sex attraction and that he was fighting a battle with pornography use.

Brodie felt she had been stopped in her tracks. She knew Greg was a little effeminate, but she never once suspected that he experienced same-sex attractions. What was she supposed to do? It sure *felt* like a big deal; was it really? Where could she go for wisdom?

Some Bible passages are cited so often that they become like a painting that's been on your wall for decades. You see it with your eyes. Yet somehow, simultaneously, you don't. It's become part of the white noise of your room. Passages of Scripture usually move to this space precisely because they are so helpful. But familiarity dulls our ability to receive them afresh.

While John 3:16 may take top trophy in this dubious competition, its nearest runner up might be Proverbs 3:5-8:

> *Trust in the LORD with all your heart,*
> *and do not lean on your own understanding.*
> *In all your ways acknowledge him,*
> *and he will make straight your paths.*
> *Be not wise in your own eyes;*
> *fear the LORD, and turn away from evil.*
> *It will be healing to your flesh*
> *and refreshment to your bones.*

If you're waiting to see how this passage is secretly about same-sex attraction, I want to be upfront: that's not what "straight" means in this passage!

That doesn't make these verses any less relevant to our topic. Over and over, like a child being taught, we need to be reminded that wisdom in the Christian life isn't found in precepts or principles. It's a person. When it comes to these kinds of practical outworkings around same-sex attracted Christians, we don't have thousands of years of pastoral guidance for living in a culture like ours. We don't have tomes of case studies. We do, however, have a living, loving God. We have his word and his Spirit. He is capable of guiding you and desirous to do so.

I've noticed considerable fear among people seeking information about dating and marrying same-sex-attracted partners: not fear of their significant other, but fear of the future. Is deciding to take this path foolish from the start? Are they dooming themselves, or their future spouse, to unhappiness or unfulfillment? Will this be the all-consuming topic of their marriage, such that it stifles other elements, like one sort of weed choking out another plant? Are they crazy for thinking that this just might work?

The hazard of writing this whole book, but especially this chapter, is that if I give you a picture of things that have worked, you might try to run out and copy it exactly, laminating it onto your life. Or you could use it as a sign to go one way or another. But I implore you: don't trust in any one story with all of your heart. Don't lean on someone else's understanding, hoping they will prepare your ways. If you want healing and refreshment, and paths that are steady and true, you have to relate to the God who made you. What is right for one couple may not be right for another, and you will need the LORD's help to determine your "straight" paths.

As Brodie considered her future with Greg, this is what she sought. Over time it was the reality of the gospel, and the Person within it, that allowed them to say yes and find a way forward.

When Greg confided in Brodie about his sexual struggles, the first thing Brodie did was thank Greg for trusting her. But next, she needed understanding: of Greg's situation and also of this phenomenon more generally. For that second one, she reached out to me and Andrew. We met halfway in Mystic, Connecticut—a historic seaport—where we talked while sitting on green grass. Andrew and I shared how our marriage was not only working in the midst of my same-sex attraction but thriving. One happy marriage doesn't make a promise of another, but I think we do need to communicate that there are many marriages like this today which are happy and normal. Which is also to say, messy.

Sometimes in the church marriage can be treated as if it's a finish line, when actually it's a type of starting gate. We don't enter into marriage and cruise; many people are surprised by how much work is needed: hence the demand for evangelical books on dating and marriage, which seems insatiable. So in

> # "Sometimes marriage can be treated as if it's a finish line, when actually it's a type of starting gate."

some ways, those entering into marriage when one person is same-sex-attracted have a leg up. They actually anticipate that sexual relationships could take work, for example! This is surely a good thing.

The peculiarity of this situation allows us to look at our potential spouse in the light of day, not just the light of infatuation, and consider, "Am I in this for the long haul?" And shouldn't all of us do this as we consider marriage? Perhaps the discernment processes in this area can help the whole church grow in entering marriages with joyful, sober thinking.

Brodie's fears were real, and common: a concern that Greg would never be truly attracted to her. A worry that sexual intimacy would be difficult, and would therefore affect other types of intimacies. She wanted to ask questions, but she also wasn't sure how much she wanted to know, which is a confusing place to be in!

There was no crystal ball to peer into, no Magic 8 Ball to shake. There were no means by which Brodie could look 15,

25, 45 years into the future and see what would happen—see if it would be worth it. None of us can. She decided that she needed to look for the gospel at work in Greg's life, and that if God was at work through grace and truth, then she could have hope.

"Trust in the LORD with all of your heart, and do not lean on your own understanding." Especially in this scenario, our understanding will be limited. We cannot truly know another person's heart. We, like Brodie, need to look for the gospel at work in our own hearts, and in the heart of our significant other, and trust the LORD to work along the rhythms of grace and truth as he always has.

In Greg, she saw that he was taking accountability seriously. That's a word as overused as the practice is underutilized—but the fruit it bears is significant. Greg took the initiative to reach out and talk about his experiences with Brodie's pastor. He sought out specialists on Christianity and same-sex attraction, to check his thinking. But most especially, he attacked his use of pornography through counseling. In Brodie's mind the attractions and the use of porn were two separate though related issues. Seeing seriousness and openness about both showed a dedication to fighting sin and temptation.

Still, there was fear. The honesty and openness were great—but would they dry up, like an over-tapped river? Over time, through prayer, through many conversations, Brodie let the gospel work in herself too. Did she see evidence of real faith in Greg? She did. Did she trust God to be her best and true husband, the one who would never leave her, the one who would care for each pain, and rejoice at each victory? Yes, she did. Brodie considered Jesus, and his goodness and faithfulness. She acknowledged that he would keep his promises and that she felt his leading toward marriage. So she decided to trust God with all her heart. God was clearly at work in Greg, and Greg was pursuing Brodie with integrity and good motives. She decided to say yes.

————

On the whole, marriage in these circumstances isn't that different from marriage between two opposite-sex-attracted people. This may come as a surprise—people assume that, because sex is such an important part of marriage, a difference here must produce a seismic shock to the system.

It is true that sex is an important aspect of marriage: important enough that if one partner is really not sexually attracted in any way to the other, marriage should not be entered into. Paul states clearly in 1 Corinthians 7:3-4, "The husband should give to his wife her conjugal rights, and likewise the wife to her husband. For the wife does not have authority over her own body, but the husband does. Likewise the husband does not have authority over his own body, but the wife does." If a potential spouse could not in good faith give their covenant partner that authority, marriage is best not entered into.

It is interesting to consider that any decision about whether or not to marry would have been unimaginable for many first-century adults. Most marriages were arranged, and husbands and wives would still have had to live in obedience to these verses, whatever their levels of sexual attraction. But those of us in cultures with elective marriage have the opportunity to weigh this element and choose the dignity of singleness or marriage.

This authority over one's body only can be granted to another in the safety of a permanent relationship of love and trust, and withholding this authority is a breach of the covenant (although there may be exceptions where a spouse is experiencing emotional or physical abuse from their partner, making sexual expression inappropriate for a time).

Now, it can happen in the course of marriage that one spouse is no longer able to perform sexually, through accident or illness perhaps. Those marriages are not in disobedience, and the Lord will provide special grace. But these exceptions do not make it safe for others to enter into marriage knowing that there is no sexual attraction.

So, yes, it is true that sex in marriage is very important. But it is also just one piece of marriage. Your marriage will suffer if you make sex the center around which everything orbits. Jesus Christ is the rightful star around which our lives

"Jesus Christ is the rightful star around which our lives and marriages must circle."

and marriages must circle; only he can properly balance the various weights of the system. Sex, money, child-rearing—all of these are normal places in which we experience tension and blessing. Crises in one area may at times create eclipses of the sun—but, like a natural eclipse, these should be rare and brief. If sexuality becomes an obsession in your marriage, you will darken the whole scene.

What are some ways this can happen? How do we discern the right difference between an unhealthy priority and proper attention to growing the sexual relationship within marriage?

First, remember that *all* marriages face some levels and seasons of sexual dysfunction. Couples in which one person is same-sex-attracted might assume that any sexual problem they experience stems from this attractional pattern. That may be the case—or it may also be a garden-variety sexual issue. For example, many couples face issues with unequal sexual desire. We often hear about husbands desiring sex more often than their wives. But I have several female friends who are in marriages where *they* desire sex more frequently than their husbands, and neither party is same-sex-attracted! It is good to know that these types of things can and do affect all kinds of couples, so that as a community in Christ we can help and support each other.

Second, you can't enter into marriage with either of you hoping that it will erase same-sex attraction. Yes, change can happen. But it is never promised. If this is a motivation for either person, you may experience bitter disappointment. It is never good for us to assume that what we want is what God provides. "Trust in the LORD with all your heart, and do not lean on your own understanding" (Proverbs 3:5). You just don't know what he has in store—it may not match your own understanding of what would be good, or fair, or right. Can you trust his character anyway?

When I was chatting with Brodie, she admitted that there was a temptation to want Greg to become straight so as to keep his eyes from straying. But, she pointed out, this is the wrong fix for what is actually a very common problem. Every married person—whatever their normal attractions—will at some point be sexually or emotionally or romantically attracted to someone who is not their spouse. Sin is "equal opportunity"—and destroying marriage, that living symbol of the gospel, is one of the devil's time-tested plays in opposing God's work in the world.

Every married person (and every unmarried person) needs to grow in fighting the temptation of lust toward someone who is not their spouse. To focus on just the same-sex attracted partner is naive. Making them straight wouldn't necessarily make them holy. Nor are they more likely to be unfaithful just because of their attractions. Every married couple is to be a team that is clear eyed about sin and hopeful in the Lord. We also need trusted brothers and sisters who help us stay faithful—it's unwise to lay that whole weight on your spouse.

Which brings us to the second thing that Brodie pointed out: trying to adjust your spouse's attractions, you seek to assume a power you don't have. You are not the Holy Spirit. You have no power to fix a result of the fall. You will never be sexy enough or romantic enough to transform desire, nor should it be your goal. Don't put your hope in those things. Put your hope in the Lord.

He is the one who will shepherd your spouse in the commitment they made to you. He is the one who will strengthen both of you to keep your vows, as you live lives of prayer, repentance, grace, and truth. "Be not wise in your own eyes; fear the LORD, and turn away from evil. It will be healing to your flesh and refreshment to your bones" (v 7-8). Do you long for true peace and healing in your relationship? The Father, Son, and Holy Spirit offer it to you; you need to reject your own wisdom and trust God's instead.

Third, don't assume that same-sex attraction is the biggest aspect of your significant other's life.

This assumption can be the result of a natural over-correction when you want to take their experience seriously. This book has covered several challenges and realities that those of us who experience same-sex attraction face. To ignore these things would be foolish and unloving! But if you're reading this book, that's probably not where you are liable to err. Instead, you may think that this is the topic that takes up their whole windshield. After all, you don't know what same-sex attraction is like firsthand, and our culture tells us that these attractions dictate most of what describes a person. But they don't.

As in any healthy dating relationship and marriage, you both need to prioritize communication. In battle, a general would be remiss to send in reinforcements, or call soldiers back from the front line, without actually having information about the battle on the ground. A coach can't make the right play calls without watching her team in real time. A parent can't choose between comfort and rebuke of his child without knowing the facts. So too, how will we know how to pray, how to encourage, how to exhort, based on assumptions alone?

Your significant other may indeed experience same-sex attraction as a primary concern. Ask how you can be helpful, and make sure you're not the only one providing support. Even then, it's possible to misjudge what type of help they actually need. If your boyfriend is wrestling with questions of identity because of his sexuality, assuming that he needs help with lust will be frustrating. If your wife is in a season of heightened same-sex temptation, counseling her about what language she should use to describe her attractions will prove exasperating. This is why educating yourself about the various ways same-sex attractions can intersect with someone's life is crucial—and why listening to your significant other carefully is so important.

But don't be surprised if in various seasons or for most of the time same-sex attraction isn't the biggest deal in your significant other's life. When I first came to Christ, this topic loomed very large. Yet for most of my marriage, it hasn't played much of a role. In the early years my more powerful temptations were around laziness, selfishness, and pride. My discipleship needs were around service, practicing humility, and things like this. It's not that my same-sex attraction disappeared. It's just that I was in a theologically secure place; the Lord had brought me much freedom to fight temptation well, and it rarely tripped me up.

Similarly, Brodie reports that when she and Greg were first married, they checked in on this topic more regularly. Over time, however, they've found they don't need to discuss it that much because it isn't the center of Greg's life. They want to maintain space to be honest about it should seasons shift. But it doesn't serve them to make this a central theme just because on a cultural level it feels as if it *should* be. They're the busy parents of three children and in full-time ministry!

Jesus hasn't called them, or us, to ignore the reality of same-sex attraction. He's also not called us to focus on it to the exclusion of other things, or when that focus is no longer needed. Only by pressing into our relationship with him— by giving life and flesh to Proverbs 3:5-8—will we grow in discerning that delicate balance.

———

I wanted to share with you Greg and Brodie's story because just having mine and Andrew's seemed too narrow. There are many couples like us flourishing today in these marriages, and I meet more all the time!

Like Brodie and Greg, Andrew and I have found our marriage remarkably *normal.* Most of our concerns are about things like raising our child, serving our church, and making sure we can make ends meet. Blissfully typical stuff. But of course, my attractions have played a part. Our process of learning healthy sexuality was bumpy—but it's hard to know how much of that was normal for early marriage and how much of it was because of my same-sex attraction.

For example, it was definitely weird getting used to Andrew's male body—so much more angular than the women I had been used to. But married sex also healed my sexuality in ways that had nothing to do with attractional patterns. As a teenager I had related to sex out of a sense of conquest, and out of the rush of the forbidden. There is nothing forbidden about married sex, no notches to add to one's belt. At first I felt lost. But slowly I discovered a healing in sex that is about saying, "I love you" again; I found a delight in the expansive permission that God gives for enjoyment of one's spouse.

Andrew certainly had to process his own internal questions as well, very similar to Brodie's: Did I really love him? Did I really desire him enough to sustain a healthy sex life? When I wasn't in the mood, was that normal and ok, or did it signal something deeper? Over time, through honest conversation and being surrounded by a healthy, Jesus-loving community, our marriage has become strong. These questions no longer badger us, because time and our actions have shown that we are for each other and love each other. There seems to be a sweet root of stability that digs deeper into the Lord every year, bearing the fruit of enjoyment and sustained commitment. May he grant us fruitfulness for the years to come.

––––––

Trusting the Lord doesn't always mean you end up married. Your significant other may be displaying ample gospel evidence in his life. You too may be seeing God work in fresh ways in your own. And yet the Lord may still be calling for you to not enter into marriage at this time—and this can happen when both partners are opposite-sex-attracted as well.

Nor does trusting the Lord mean that if he leads you into marriage, it will be cheery and free of trouble. Marriage is not the goal of the Christian life or its promised rest. Jesus is the goal; Jesus is our rest. We have been formed by a culture in love with romance and sex but not in love with our Creator. We have to constantly poke at our expectations, our hopes, and our fears.

Some of you reading this are already in a marriage to someone who is same-sex-attracted, and are experiencing very tough realities. If this is you, you must seek support and help. Don't suffer in silence. Marriage is one of the most beautiful gifts God has given to us and is a frequent place for attack.

Our own sin, the brokenness of the world, the evil desires of spiritual adversaries all assail our marriages like a barrage of missiles against a city. You must seek refuge in the means God has provided—his Spirit, his word, and his people. Especially in crisis, Christian counseling is a wise and godly move.

Trusting the Lord can't be reduced to a flow chart, a magic charm, or a checklist. It flows from a relationship with a Person; you have to seek him first and rely on him. He has established many marriages where same-sex attraction exists and has caused them to flourish under his care. I write from such a one, and have seen others with my own eyes, like that of Brodie and Greg. You are not foolish to think that it could work for you! You are only foolish to not seek his specific direction, wherever he may lead.

> *Trust in the LORD with all your heart,*
> *and do not lean on your own understanding.*
> *In all your ways acknowledge him,*
> *and he will make straight your paths.*
> *Be not wise in your own eyes;*
> *fear the LORD, and turn away from evil.*
> *It will be healing to your flesh*
> *and refreshment to your bones. (Proverbs 3:5-8)*

CHAPTER 9

UNEXPECTED
IDENTITY

Emily knew she was gay at age 14.

She grew up in North London in a supportive, atheistic family, so her discovery of her sexuality was not overly stressful. "The way my friends talked about boys didn't seem to match how I felt," she remembers. "They would hang out of the school-room windows and catcall the boys on the street outside! And I had absolutely no interest." She didn't jump to any quick conclusions, but by early adolescence the way she noticed other young women seemed to match the language of her friends' crushes on young men. And these weren't one-off notices. Her attractions manifested themselves in what she calls a "settled pattern."

She had her first girlfriend at around the age of 15 or 16, and decided at that point to come out to her family. They responded with love, joy, and acceptance. Although Emily's first relationship soon ended in a broken teenaged heart, having her sexuality affirmed by her friends and family was a positive experience overall. There was no shame about being gay, and no doubt. Whatever weirdness first manifested itself in her friendship group dissipated quickly. It was a liberal all-girls school, and her classmates weren't ones to be shocked for long.

And so, as a teenager getting ready to head off to the University of Bristol, Emily says she was certain and comfortable with how to describe herself. She was "gay."

During her time at university, Emily got very involved with student theater. While working on a production of *The Taming of the Shrew*, a conversation with one of her new friends took a strange turn: "My friend sneezed, and I politely said 'Bless you.' She turned round and asked, 'Who are you asking to bless me?'"

From there began a series of spiritual conversations, leading to Emily's friend giving her a Bible with favorite passages marked up. Now, Emily knew that Christianity was not accepting of same-gender romantic relationships, even though she had never officially heard that taught, nor had she been mistreated by a Christian. Even so, what she encountered in the Bible moved her deeply. Though she hadn't considered the Christian faith much before in her life, suddenly she was thinking about it quite a lot!

Reading about Mary hearing the resurrected Jesus call her name in the garden, Emily couldn't help but want to pray—but to whom? The Spirit continued to stir her. She began attending an Alpha course, where one evening she heard about the coming banquet of heaven, where all of God's people will be gathered to enjoy him and each other forever. "I just remember thinking, *'Yes, I want to be there!'*"

Now she had a new word to describe herself. She was a Christian.

———

You may have noticed several similarities between Emily's story and mine, but perhaps the most significant one is this: we were both women who discovered and came to terms with our attractional patterns while we were *outside of the church*. I'm convinced that for both of us, being able to identify our attractions without shame early on has helped us to process them later in a healthy way in Christ. By contrast, many people who grew up in the church did not find it to be a safe place in which to discuss same-sex attraction, let alone admit to experiencing it.

This should not be. If a person can't acknowledge their same-sex attraction in the church, how can they get the pastoral care and guidance that they need? More than that, we owe it to the world to communicate God's vision for sex and

"Shouldn't the guides own the best maps?"

gender with grace, clarity, and wisdom, so that we might fulfill our mission to make disciples in our generation. Without proper equipping, we will simply cede the conversation to our culture. Shouldn't the guides own the best maps?

To be reliable guides, we need to better understand the terrain around two pressing topics in the conversation around sexuality today. First, how stable are same-sex attractions? And second, what role do or should they play in the formation of a person's identity, especially when it comes to the labels we choose? The first will naturally shape the second: our conclusion about how sexual attraction relates to our essential selves will influence our language choices, as well as how we evaluate the choices of others.

———

The common narrative in the LGBT+ community is that one is born same-sex attracted and that can never change. That makes intuitive sense for most of us who found that these attractions arose unasked for—spontaneously, strongly, enduringly. And since this is the case, choosing the label of gay or lesbian seems as normal as calling myself American because of where I was born.

But this leads to an interesting pastoral phenomenon. I have been doing campus-ministry work for over a decade and have at various times been approached by nervous men and women who have confided in me that they experience some amount of same-sex attraction. And over and over again I have been asked, "Does this mean I'm gay?"

They're not asking a nonsensical question. So much of the cultural drive recently has been to assert that if you have these attractions, then you must name them and base your identity on them. Not to do so is to live in the closet: a place of shame and woe. My students naturally want to know, if these attractions are true some of the time, whether it makes best sense to adopt a queer identity?

Even for those outside of the church, however, the picture is more nuanced than popular culture would suggest. In 2008, the atheist lesbian academic Lisa Diamond published *Sexual Fluidity: Understanding Women's Love and Desire*, based on a ten-year study of 100 women and their reports on attractional patterns and identity choices. She initially had women choose a word for themselves: straight, lesbian, bisexual or unlabeled. She reports, "I was struck, at that first interview, by the amount of self-reflection involved in women's selection of that initial identity." The women had done a deep amount of soul-searching to come up with their word. How much same-sex attraction does one need to identify as bi or lesbian? How strong do the attractions need to be? Does one attraction "count"? What makes something a fluke?

The reason Diamond's women were so careful was because wearing any word in the world but "straight" carries all kinds of real-life consequences. For some it brings real danger. It can change how others see you—perhaps even how you see yourself. True, assuming a non-straight identity has become safer and more normal in certain locations since Diamond's study—large Western metropolitan areas or liberal college campuses for example. Yet the process of analyzing your attractions and figuring out if—and how—you want to identify by them can still be a fraught task.

In her 2008 book, Diamond reported that a large swath of her women ended up changing the labels they used for themselves. This happened least among those who could be called "very straight" or "very lesbian," but many women who report some same-sex attraction do not actually fit into this latter category. Diamond specifically noted that "when women undertook identity changes, they typically did so in a way that broadened rather than narrowed their potential range of attractions and relationships" (*Sexual Fluidity*, p 67).

Over a decade later, the trend away from highly defined, and therefore limited, words like gay and lesbian has continued. Particularly among young people, there is now a growing preference for open-ended descriptions like "pansexual"— describing someone whose attractions are not limited with regard to biological sex or gender. Indeed, as Diamond reflected in her book, "one of the most fascinating findings of the study was the fact that many women dealt with the perceived fluidity and unpredictability of their sexuality by casting off all identity labels" (*Sexual Fluidity*, p 74).

And this is probably why many people who experience what they would consider to be a small amount or an unpredictable pattern of same-sex attraction don't choose to identify based on it. In fact, Diamond puts it more starkly: "Most individuals with same-sex attractions do not publicly identify themselves as lesbian/gay/bisexual" (*Sexual Fluidity*, p 27). But in our hyper-individualized and hyper-sexualized culture, there is more and more pressure to give a name to and identify with our sexual feelings—even as the number of available "names" has expanded.

What does this mean for Christians who want to live well and minister well? For starters, we need to recognize that same-sex attraction is much more prevalent in the population than previously acknowledged. Anytime we discuss experiencing same-sex attraction as a Christian, we are helping more than just the small percentage of us who have exclusive or near-exclusive attractions.

It also means that our culture's move away from narrow identity-markers could actually prove helpful for articulating the Christian worldview. There's now a visible precedent for experiencing real same-sex attraction and yet choosing to describe it in ways that aren't so tied up with our identity.

So our culture is shifting—but what does the Bible say? Does the real experience of same-sex attraction have the last word on who we authentically are? How are we meant to think and talk about ourselves in relationship to these things?

Let's ask the apostle Paul.

———

The Galatian church was made of non-Jewish people in the main, who had accepted the gospel but then succumbed to pressure to practice Jewish customs. They were led to believe that salvation required acceptance of Jesus Christ *plus* Jewish observance. God wouldn't be pleased by faith alone, but by faith plus the law. Paul's letter to the Galatians is a forthright take-down of this heresy.

Never does Paul argue that the law is evil; he is clear in Galatians 3:21-24 that the law is good and served a good purpose. But it could not save us. Otherwise Jesus would not have needed to die for our sake! The law served as a guardian until he came. Paul concludes:

> ^{25} *But now that faith has come, we are no longer under*
> *a guardian, ^{26} for in Christ Jesus you are all sons of God,*
> *through faith. ^{27} For as many of you as were baptized into*
> *Christ have put on Christ. ^{28} There is neither Jew nor Greek,*
> *there is neither slave nor free, there is no male and female,*
> *for you are all one in Christ Jesus. ^{29} And if you are Christ's,*
> *then you are Abraham's offspring, heirs according to promise.*
> *(Galatians 3:25-29)*

Our eyes and hearts immediately are pulled toward 3:28; it's bold, famous, and recently somewhat controversial. But notice how the overall theme of the paragraph is the reality of *family*. The Galatians wanted to be sure they *really were* God's people, hence the pressure to adopt Jewish forms of religion. Yet Paul's reassurance is that they are *already* in the family! Already sons of God, already Abraham's famous offspring.

And the mechanism for getting there isn't observance of the law. It is all through Jesus Christ's perfect obedience even unto death. The language is so immersive: if by faith we receive his righteousness, we enter *in* to Christ (v 26). We are literally owned by him. We don't own us; our friends don't own us; our families don't own us; our attractions don't own us. Only Jesus owns us.

I especially love Paul's use of the phrase in verse 27: we "have put on Christ." That is a great English translation of a single Greek verb which most typically refers to the everyday act of putting on your clothes. Clothes have always been a key way to signal things about ourselves. Think of how all the best high-school movies signal the various subcultures through clothing choice. Jocks wear some things; goths wear others. The protagonist often goes through a dramatic transformation, signaled by a complete change in their clothing and style, as in the 1999 classic *She's All That*. There's something so *fitting* about our clothes reflecting who we are.

How natural, then, that Paul uses the word "put on" for those of us who belong wholly and fully to Jesus. Whatever our circumstances, our gifts or our background, we "wear" Jesus wherever we go. We don't need to become Jews, or straight, to enter into the family of God. By faith, we have full access to forgiveness, acceptance, and transformation into the likeness of our big brother Christ.

This is the context for the famous words of Galatians 3:28: "There is neither Jew nor Greek, there is neither slave nor free, there is no male and female, for you are all one in Christ Jesus." Paul isn't saying that these categories literally don't exist; throughout his letters he refers to all six of these types of people specifically. Nor does he suggest that these qualities are meaningless now in Christ or unimportant. The whole letter is about Gentiles being allowed to be Gentiles, though transformed in Christ! Other texts such as Ephesians 5:22 – 6:9, which gives specific instructions to husbands and wives, and slaves and masters, show clearly that these categories impact how we live our Christian lives.

What is he saying, then? Simply that our identity as Christians—and, more to the point, our *unity* as Christians—is more fundamental than even these things that are true and important about ourselves.

Now, it's important to point out that *some* things that are true and important about us are morally neutral and unchangeable, like our sex and nationality. It's no result of the fall that I am female and not Jewish, though I could always choose to wield these realities in ways that are fallen.

But other things that are true and important about us *are* fallen, or morally problematic. They may exist on a sliding scale from transience and permanence, like the experience of ancient slavery and freedom. Nonetheless, for us to relate to these things well, it is helpful to acknowledge them.

Same-sex attractions are in this second category. They are

true in the sense that they exist. They are important, especially because the culture presses us to treat them as safe and good while Scripture presses us to soberly flee temptation of all kinds. They must be denied, in the sense that we must say no to their demands for same-gender sex and romance. But they need *not* be denied in the sense of going unacknowledged. We can't make war with an opponent while stopping our eyes and ears to their whereabouts.

We shouldn't pretend that our same-sex attraction—as with all the realities listed in Galatians 3:28—doesn't impact our Christian life and discipleship, often profoundly. But Paul is saying that *everything* about us moves underneath the reality of being united with others into Jesus, into God's family. This is the main thing about us—plural intended.

———

This intersection between identity and attractions is one that Emily, who we met at the start of the chapter, has wrestled over.

She remembers, as a new Christian, going to a talk on gender roles and walking away with a profound conviction. She remembers thinking, "Wow—my identity in Christ may be calling me to a new identity in everything."

She stood on a street corner, feeling overwhelmed that her sexuality didn't seem to fit her new identity—that is, she knew she couldn't give it expression as she had freely done before. No more sexual and romantic relationships with women. "Walking home, with tears streaking down my face, I realized both that I could spend my entire life single as a result of that fact and that it would still be worth it. I said to myself, 'I love Jesus more.'"

She's been saying that ever since. In those early years, the language she used to describe herself was, "I'm gay, but I'm a Christian." She acknowledged the attractions but anchored her choices and identity elsewhere. Eventually she found she had to come out to her family again—this time as a Christian!

If anything they found this more difficult to accept—but they saw that Emily was happy, and were happy for her.

Then suddenly, Emily's attractions completely changed.

At first, she kept it to herself. It was just so surprising—she had never asked for a change nor expected it. And it wasn't as if she had formed a relational attachment to a man, and then it grew into something else. No. Simply on a set one day, she realized that she—to use her British expression—"fancied this younger bloke." It completely caught her off guard. That had never happened before. But it persisted. Maybe it was just a one-off fluke?

Indeed not. Soon it became clear that her attractions were for men, almost exclusively—over a decade later, she estimates that 98-99% of any particular attractions she feels are now towards men.

At first, her emotions were all over the place. It was just, well, weird. She didn't feel sorrow at the change, but she did have to process it. She wondered, "Who does that mean that I am?" Did this change mean that she was "fake gay" before? No, that didn't seem right at all. Her attraction and relationships with women were very real and undeniable. It wasn't as if her opposite-sex attractions had simply been hiding. No, these attractions toward men arose just as spontaneously and as enduringly as her previous same-sex attractions.

When I ask what language she uses for herself now, it's clear that it's complicated. She sounds a lot like Lisa Diamond's women who cast off identity labels as more trouble than they were worth. Emily really just wants to be known as a Christian: "I stopped wanting to describe myself in the ways I had before."

What are we to make of a story like Emily's? For one thing it demonstrates, in flesh and blood, just how closely entwined the subjects of attraction change and identity are. What you assert in one topic makes claims in the other. And it's foolish—dangerous—to pretend that these conversations don't already have a history with each other. On their own, they can stir up plenty of internet dust. Combine them, and this can swirl into a tornado.

They're never just topics, of course. Real people have been caught in the cross-fire between competing assumptions and assertions around identity and change. For men and women who grew up in the church in the 1980s, 90s, and beyond, same-sex attraction was largely cast as utter perversion that was actively chosen in order to demonstrate hatred for God. A person would only identify as gay if they had given up on Christianity. So if you experienced same-sex attraction but loved Jesus, you usually kept dead quiet or actively sought to "pray the gay away," or both. It was often a lonely, dark experience. People spent earnest, tear-soaked years begging God to change them, only to find he didn't—and that most of their contemporaries experienced no lasting change either.

And yet even this is not the *only* narrative. True, what is known as "reparative therapy," a program which aims to "create" heterosexuality, is a false gospel—it makes promises God does not and is not even scientifically valid, let alone biblically valid. It blames same-sex attraction on various environmental factors—even on the person who doesn't want those attractions—leading to an endless search for *why* instead of equipping to fight the *what*. But at the same time, some people who experienced reparative therapy insist that though its aims were faulty, they still found help in the process. They made good friendships and did gain ground in obeying God instead of their desires. Some found it to be the only place where they could discuss being a Christian who experienced these attractions without being ridiculed or distrusted.

Does their positive experience cancel out the negative ones? Does Emily's experience of total, unasked-for change somehow support looking for that for others? Does my being married mean that that should be a goal for everyone?

No, and no, and no.

As I've already said, the danger in telling just one story is that there isn't just one story. And *your* story is only fully known to the Lord. What does it mean for you to fight temptation, choose holiness, and relate to the topics of attraction change and identity? Of course, there are some things that it has to mean because they're laid out in God's word. But there are other things which will look different for each of us.

With God in the picture, unexpected things can and do happen. He is always working for the transformation of his people; he is always equipping us to fight sin and pursue

"With God in the picture, unexpected things can and do happen. We simply can't put him in a box."

him in holiness. Sometimes that means allowing people who earnestly seek change to find it—or not. Sometimes it means bringing dramatic or subtle change to those who didn't care if it ever happened—or not. We simply can't put God in a box.

You may be sure in your bones that your patterns will never change; indeed, you may be right! The best evidence indicates that, especially for those who experience near-exclusive opposite- or same-sex attractions, those patterns don't change. Yet there is more than one Emily in the world. Or even if your patterns don't change, God could bring about different surprises, like an attraction toward the one opposite-sex person he calls you to marry.

You might find this final detail from Emily's story unexpected too: though her attractions have been for men for many years now, that hasn't at this point led to marriage. Like many singles, she has wrestled with times of discontentment, asking God, "Well, if you're going to provide the change, what for?!" And yet that same memory of tearful surrender returns to her again and again. Whatever her attractions, Jesus is still precious, beautiful, and worthy. He is the pearl of great price: more desirable even than a happy marriage. Emily continues to find her hope in the Lord who loves her.

And what then about the language question? Should you call yourself a "gay Christian"? Or should you instead use language like "same-sex-attracted"? Some argue that the former is a category error—that to use words like "gay" in conjunction with "Christian" automatically places sin into one's core identity, in utter conflict with the righteousness we are called to in Jesus. Yet others, who likewise hold to God's sexual ethic, say that it is the best language they know of to communicate their experience of attraction accurately. Some would also argue that "same-sex-attracted" is bulky, sounds unnecessarily strange in our wider culture, and, for some, is connected with the difficult era of reparative therapy.

So what are we to conclude? As we consider our relationship to our same-sex attractions and what it means for our identity, we should be primarily concerned with how it interacts with the feedback loop of how we relate to God and how we see ourselves. Remember, as Paul would counsel, that there are many true things about us which don't need to be denied. But at the same time, our primary identity is as a member of the family of God. Which language best promotes the battle with same-sex sin? Which promotes robust love for Jesus Christ? Which language best promotes unity of the body and mutual understanding? Which best assists you in sharing the gospel in our culture?

As I've already suggested, women and men who love Jesus and his word come down slightly differently on the best answers to these questions. Personally, I find most help in terms like "same-sex attraction" for my experience. Though that phrase does have a hard history in relations to people who were caught up in the reparative therapy movement, on the whole, I find it communicates well with the church and the world, and helps me dissociate from the life I used to live. My attractions are true about me—I don't need to hide them, but only fight them when they rear up. But they do not own me; Jesus does.

I worry that calling oneself a gay or queer Christian creates too much opportunity for this part of our lives to shape our identities in ways that are unhelpful—to perhaps close us off from things God may want to do, or allow types of compromise with attraction. It's all too easy to slide from recognizing something as true about myself to seeing it as *the* truth about myself. I want us to be sober and watchful in our language choices.

But above all else, I want us to be charitable to ourselves and toward each other. The stories of what God is doing may surprise, delight, or alarm us. Let's listen to each other rather than shutting one another down. Let's admonish one another in love, rather than firing shots at each other on social media. Let's warn each other of sin, and point each other to the confounding grace of our Savior, rather than condemning one another as heretics or Pharisees without so much as a trial.

Jesus Christ has clothed us and possessed us, and our identity is in him, as his family—together. Whatever our attraction changes or language choices, he will surely complete the work he has begun.

EPILOGUE

"I've just never met anyone else like this, like me, before."

Whenever I hear a statement like this from a same-sex-attracted Christian, I remember feeling the same near the start of my journey—as if I was the only Christian in the world who was battling this. There can be a strange loneliness in not knowing anyone else who experiences this specific reality. Having no role models amplifies our questions. Will these desires prove too formidable for me—will I eventually give in? Are they here just to be survived or do they serve a greater purpose as well? Will I be alone, forever lonely? What comes next, and next, and next?

I wrote this book to begin to answer some of these questions. But the truth is that we'll always be left with more questions. The realities of our individual situations are too different, and too messy, for me to possibly address every specific aspect. That's why, as we finish, I want to leave you not with answers but with three promises from the One who loves us—the One who makes this all worthwhile. These are promises which hold true for every believer, whoever we are and whatever our desires and wherever we find ourselves.

Jesus promises that you have his power—even right in your weakness. He died so that he alone would own you. He rose to gift you his Spirit, who is always ready to empower you for the fight. Though these desires are real, they do not define you. Though God's enemy can use them to strategize against you, you serve under a greater General with greater weapons. This can be seen even more clearly as you watch those ahead of you in the fight.

Jesus promises that you have companions. Maybe you have left same-sex romance and remember its contours well. Or you've never tasted it, and that absence creates a void which the imagination runs wild to fill. Yet we've seen that the church is meant to be, and can be, family. We've seen that same-sex friendship in the Lord is meant to be wisely and joyfully embraced as a place of rightful intimacy. We've seen that God will call some of us into marriage, perhaps to our great surprise, and that we don't have to "become straight" to receive that gift. Certainly, each of these types of relationship will be imperfect here—but that doesn't make them less valuable. They are worth striving for.

Jesus promises that you have a purpose. Your attractions may be a result of the fall, but God has made us more than conquerors (Romans 8:37). Both locally and within our wider Christian culture, believers with same-sex attractions can teach the church about desire, about faithfulness, and about healthy relationships. You can show the church costly obedience that glorifies the Lord. And you can show your community how precious Christ is. You can confound the world with answers and questions it never expected—one friend or coworker or neighbor at a time. You can share the gospel through the very thing that seems most offensive and bizarre about you—your refusal to take your desires more seriously than your God. I hope the stories in this book have given you a glimpse of how this can work: that it is both possible and dazzling.

For every Christian, not least those who experience same-sex attraction, God has promised "a future and a hope" (Jeremiah 29:11). When the prophet Jeremiah spoke these words to ancient Israel, he spoke to them as a unit, as a nation. It was not an individualistic promise, and certainly not spoken to *them* so that *we* could one day slap it on kitsch graduation gifts. No, these words were spoken to a nation who had just experienced the brutality of a foreign invasion—to a people facing decades in exile in Babylon under God's judgment for their sins.

Yet in the midst of that pain and disgrace, God promised he would one day take his people out of shame and into new life; he would one day bring them back home. So he told them to plant and build and marry while they waited in Babylon for what he would surely do: "Build houses and live in them; plant gardens and eat their produce. Take wives and have sons and daughters" (v 5-6).

We who experience same-sex attraction have not been dragged off to a literal Babylon. Yet there has been pain—sometimes because of our sin, and sometimes because of exile and exclusion. We are still in the midst of that. Like all other Christians we have not yet been brought to our land of rest.

"In Jesus we are God's people: beloved, and gathered, and seen."

And though we are not the physical nation of Israel, in Jesus we are God's people: beloved, and gathered, and seen. We can plant and build, and, yes, sometimes even marry, while we wait for what Christ will bring to completion in the new creation. There is life for us now, and forever.

We have no shame which he was not willing to put on his own back and bear away. We have no sin that his blood doesn't drown. Because of his work and his love, we do have a future and hope that outstrips our past and present. We will be oaks of righteousness, planted in his groves, fruitfully beautiful under his care.

ACKNOWLEDGMENTS

I thank God in Christ for all of the people who helped bring this book into the world. May it bring him glory and build his church.

If Ella and Phil Kenney hadn't provided preschool for my daughter, I would have had no time to write in the midst of my other responsibilities. Trillia Newbell, during our very first lunch together, believed in what I was casting vision for and connected me to The Good Book Company.

Carl Laferton took my meandering description of what I thought would bless same-sex attracted Christians and reflected it back to me in a coherent concept. I was strengthened by the fact that he believed in the project so quickly and joyfully. Rachel Jones consistently provided me with encouragement, as well as excellent edits that not only improved my manuscript but did so in my own voice. She has perhaps ruined me for any other editor. Don Gates has been an advocate and source of enthusiasm and guidance.

Several friends read the manuscript in whole or in part. Rebecca McLaughlin actively edited every stitch of this book, always making me sound better. She almost seemed to will the book into existence through her sheer desire for it—calling for it and believing in it before even I did. Ed, Emily, Greg and Brodie took the risk of being vulnerable in someone else's book, handing me the responsibility and privilege of sharing their stories. This book would be so much less without each of them. Sam Allberry beautifully took up the tone and mission of this work, adding lift and strength right at the starting gate. I'm honored to have his words lead into my own.

It's one thing to put my own story out there. But without Andrew's belief and support, and his willingness to have part of his own story told, this project never would have gotten off the ground. For more than a decade he has shown a deep commitment to God's work through me, which is a deep source of strength and security.

Finally, the way my daughter delights in the fact that I am an author brings me great joy. She soberly counseled me to "not write any more articles, but only books. Hundreds of books." I'm not sure I'll take her advice.

the good book
COMPANY

BIBLICAL | RELEVANT | ACCESSIBLE

At The Good Book Company, we are dedicated to helping Christians and local churches grow. We believe that God's growth process always starts with hearing clearly what he has said to us through his timeless word—the Bible.

Ever since we opened our doors in 1991, we have been striving to produce Bible-based resources that bring glory to God. We have grown to become an international provider of user-friendly resources to the Christian community, with believers of all backgrounds and denominations using our books, Bible studies, devotionals, evangelistic resources, and DVD-based courses.

We want to equip ordinary Christians to live for Christ day by day, and churches to grow in their knowledge of God, their love for one another, and the effectiveness of their outreach.

Call us for a discussion of your needs or visit one of our local websites for more information on the resources and services we provide.

Your friends at The Good Book Company

thegoodbook.com | thegoodbook.co.uk
thegoodbook.com.au | thegoodbook.co.nz
thegoodbook.co.in